The Artworks of Eugene J. Martin in the Private Art Collection of Isabel and David Taylor

Suzanne Fredericq

ISBN: 978-0-578-02940-5

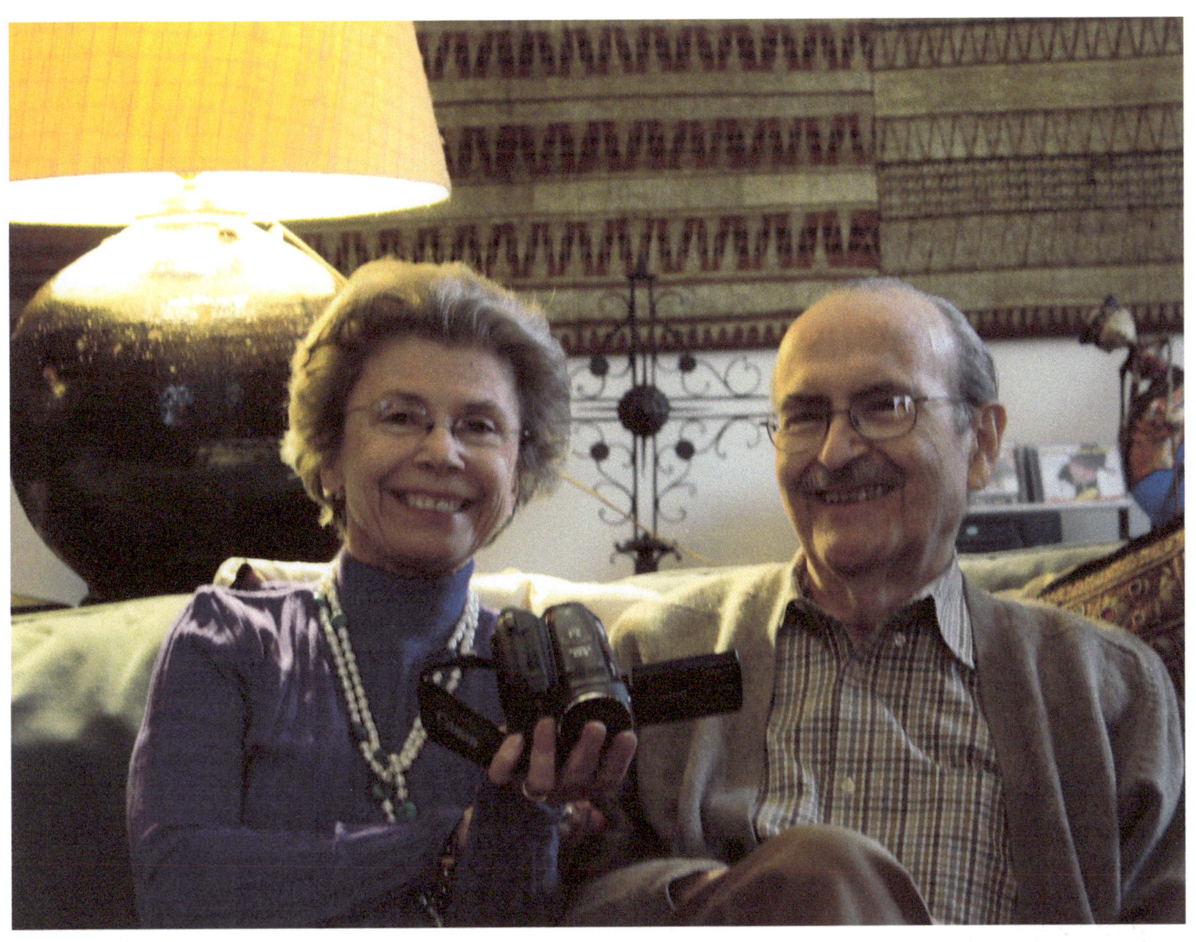

Isabel and David Taylor in their living room in Washington D.C., January 2009

Foreword

We have lived with Eugene J. Martin for many years, starting in 1975 when he moved into the basement apartment in our house in Spring Valley, Washington, D.C. We began to collect his drawings and paintings at that time.

Our collection has grown and covers many of the important parts of the walls of our present apartment in the Woodley Park Towers, near the National Zoo, in Washington DC.

David says: "When I eat at my place at the kitchen table my eye keeps fixating upon "The Open Door," which is also Isabel's favorite painting! "When I work at my desk in my bedroom the same is true with respect to "The New Yorker."

Wherever one turns, almost, one's eye feasts upon a drawing or painting by Eugene. It is a never-ending joy for the body, memory and soul.

Eugene was a good friend, with whom we spent much relevant time, and whose art has graced our lives.

Eugene is always with us, he lives through his art.

Isabel and David Taylor,
Washington D.C., June 17, 2009

I still remember the day as if it were yesterday. A balmy Spring day in Georgetown, Washington D.C., March 1982. There, on a low table in the house of a mutual friend laid a stack of pencil drawings. Drawings by an artist who signed them E.J. Martin. I fell in love with these drawings before I met and fell in love with the person.

It was on that balmy Spring day when Eugene Martin came to visit his friend Isabel Taylor in the house in Georgetown. That day I happened to be there as well. And that day I fell in love with the person.

Suzanne Fredericq,

Lafayette, Louisiana, June 17, 2009

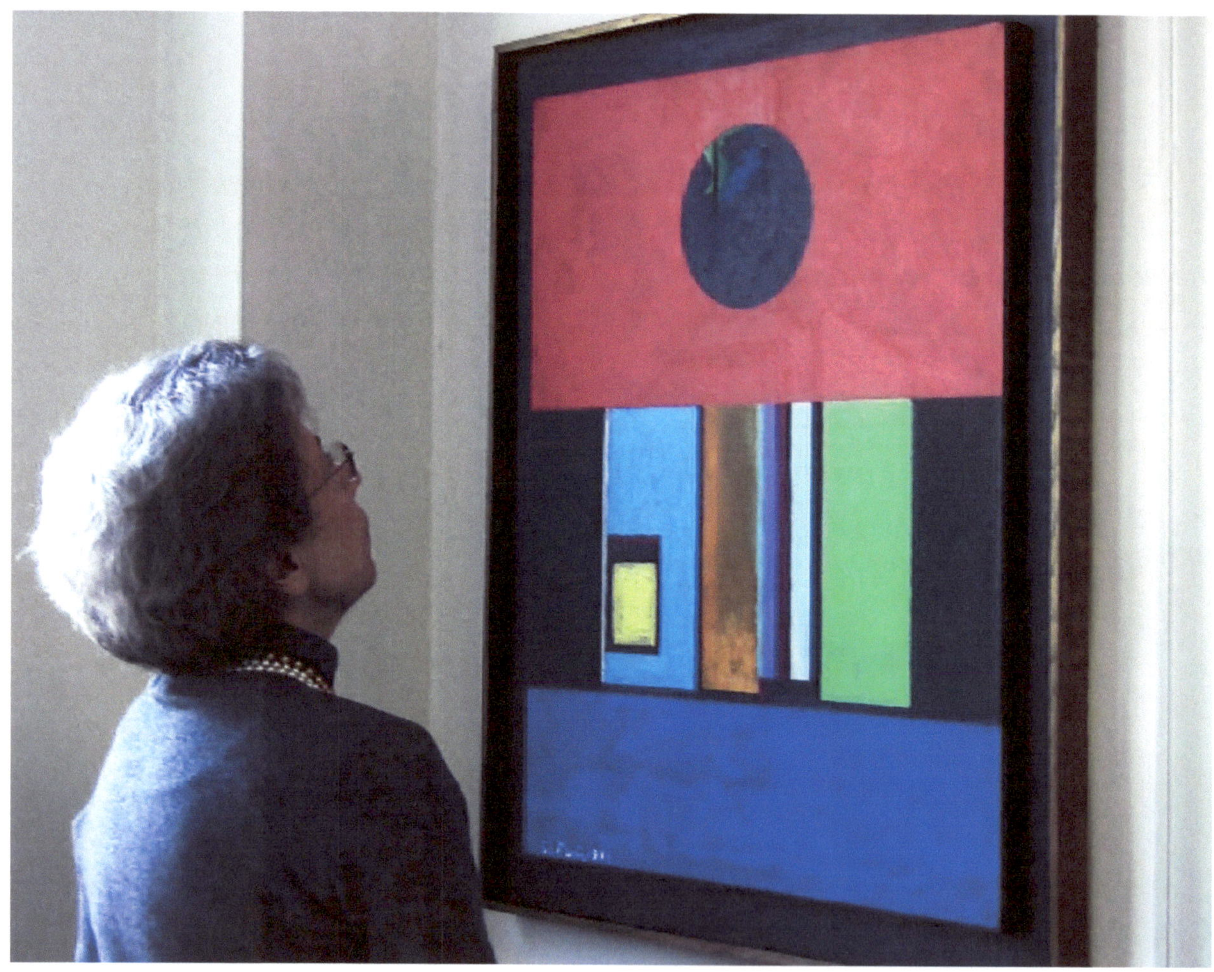

Isabel Taylor in front of "The Open Door", her favorite Eugene Martin painting; acrylic on canvas, 1994

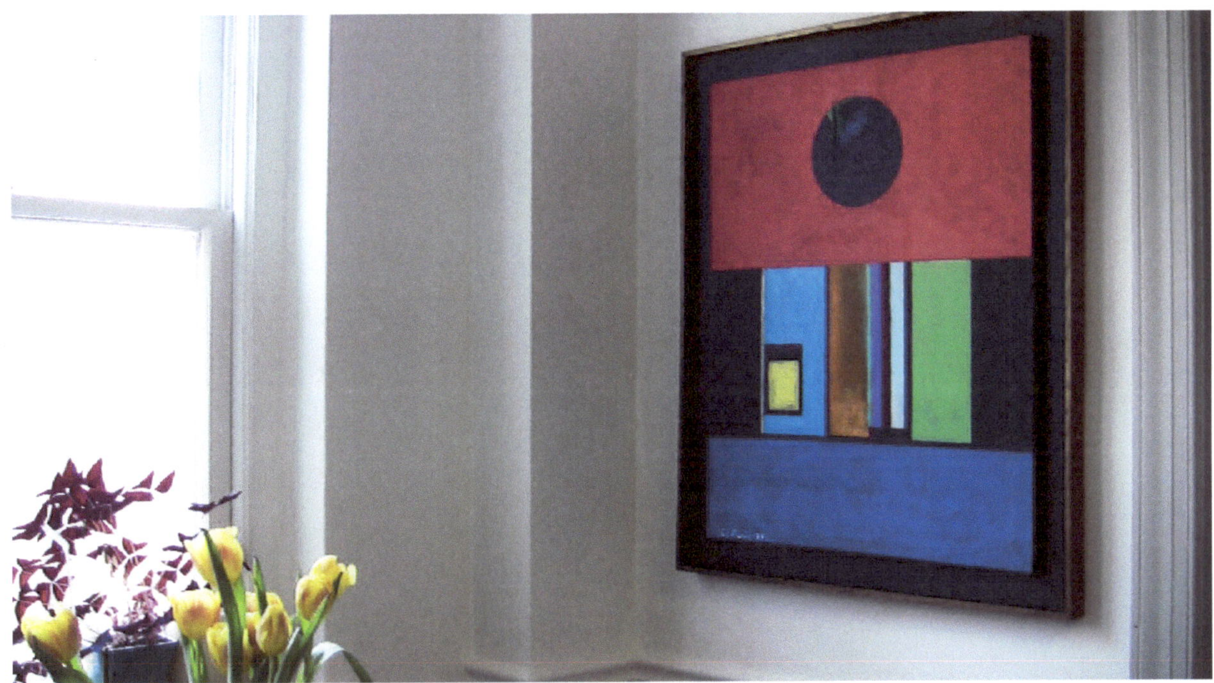

View from the kitchen; "The Open Door," acrylic on canvas, 1994

Detail of "The Open Door," acrylic painting on canvas, 1994

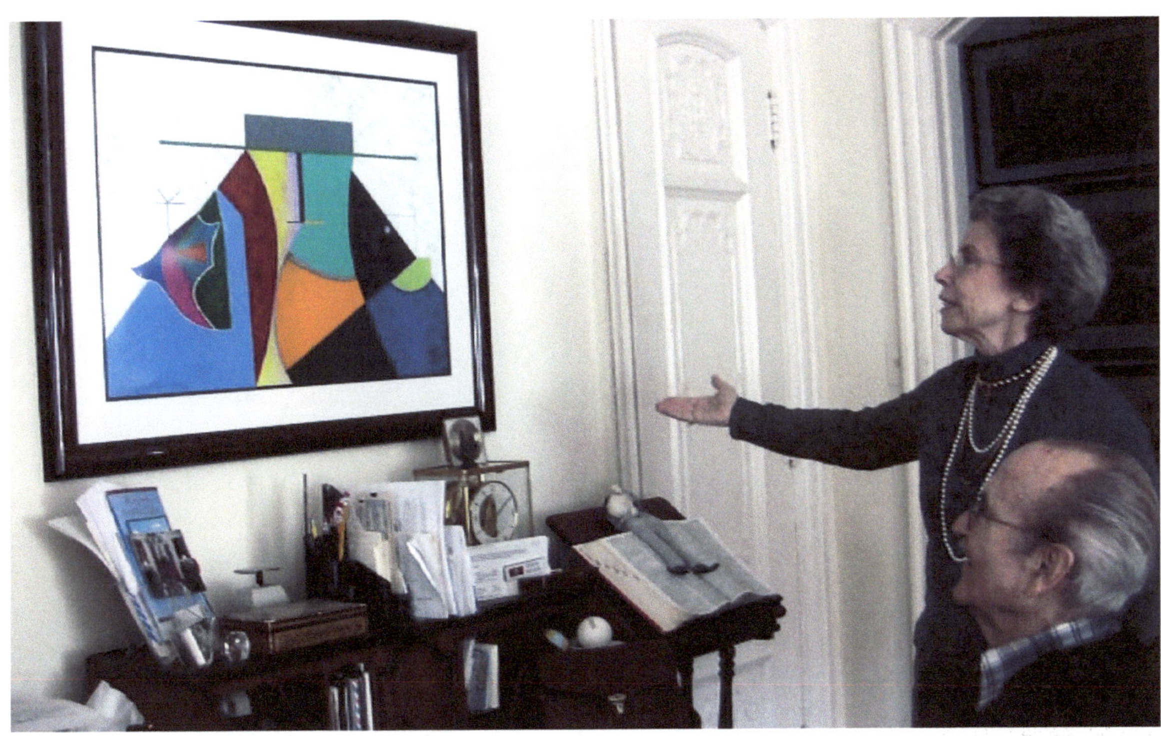

Isabel and David Taylor enjoy looking at "The New Yorker," acrylic painting on paper, 1992.

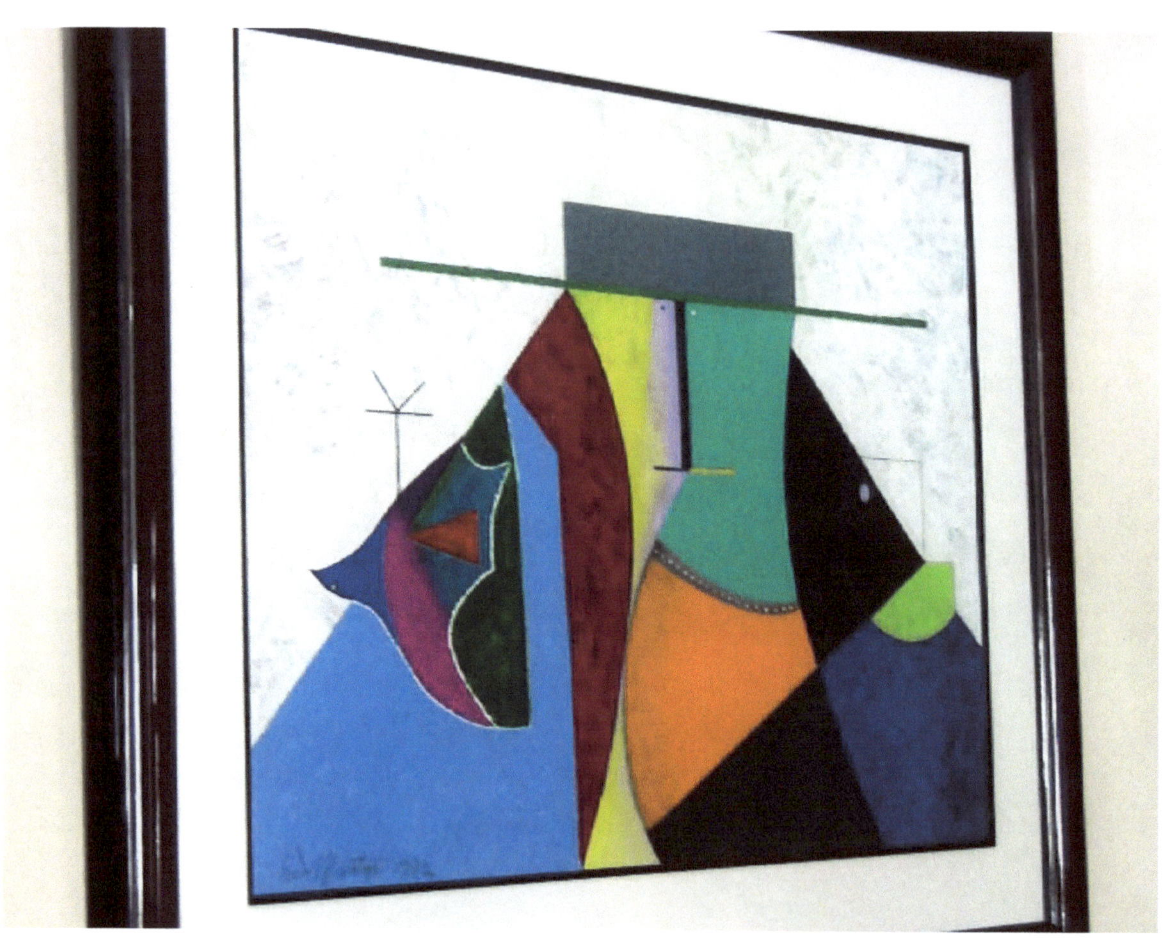

"The New Yorker," acrylic painting on paper, 1992, hanging in David Taylor's office in his apartment in Washington D.C.

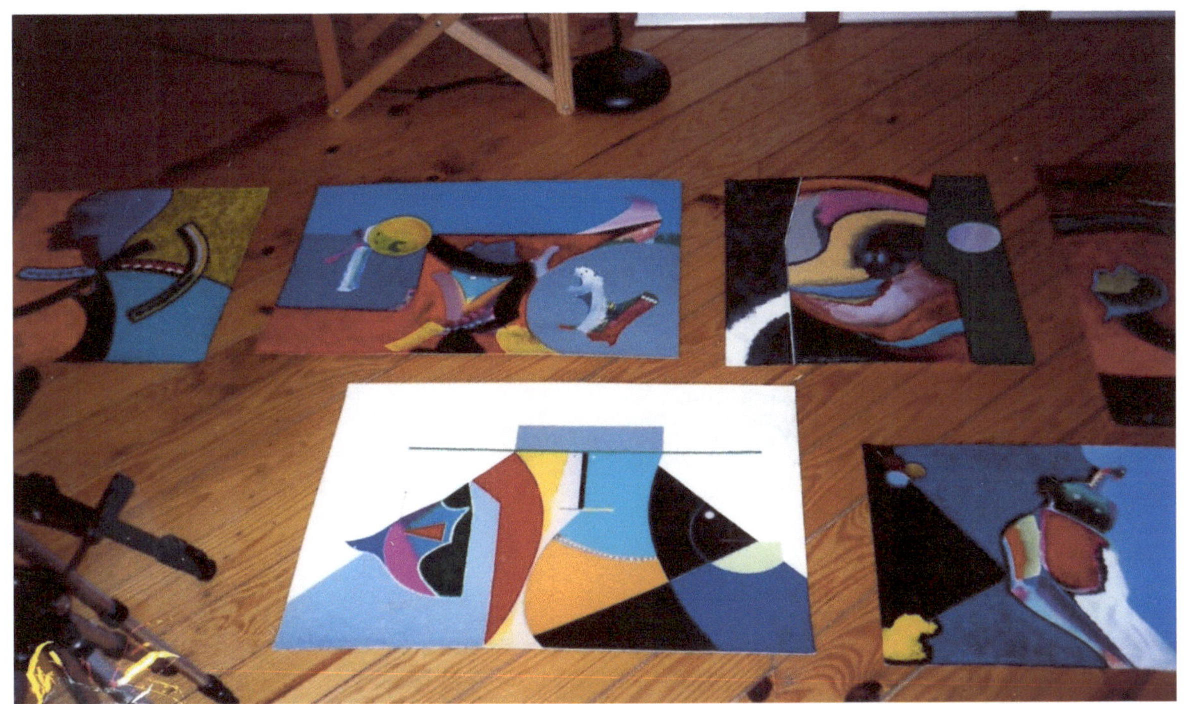

"The New Yorker" among other acrylic works on paper spread out on the floor in Eugene Martin's studio in Washington D.C., 1992

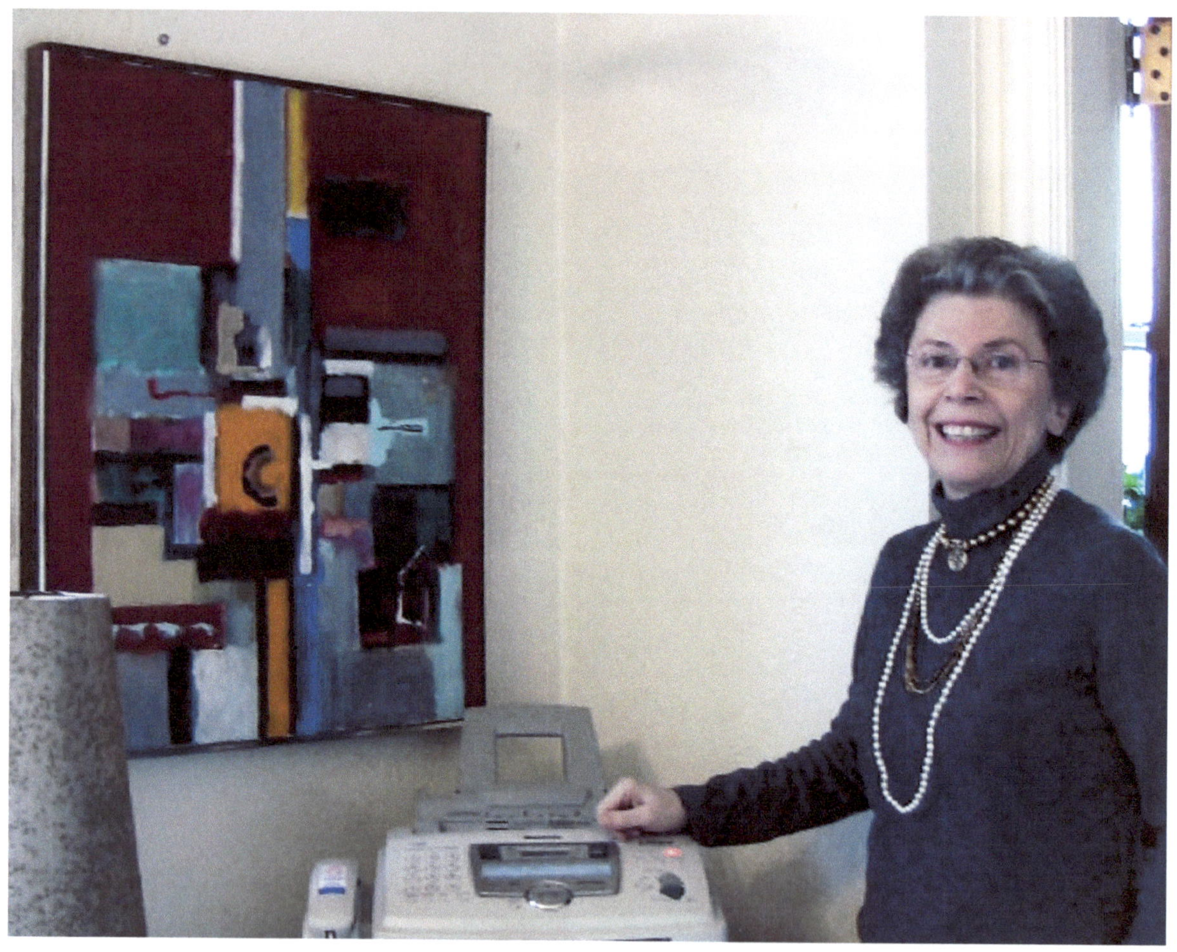

"The Mustard Seed", acrylic painting on canvas, 1981, hanging in the studio office of Isabel Taylor in Washington D.C.

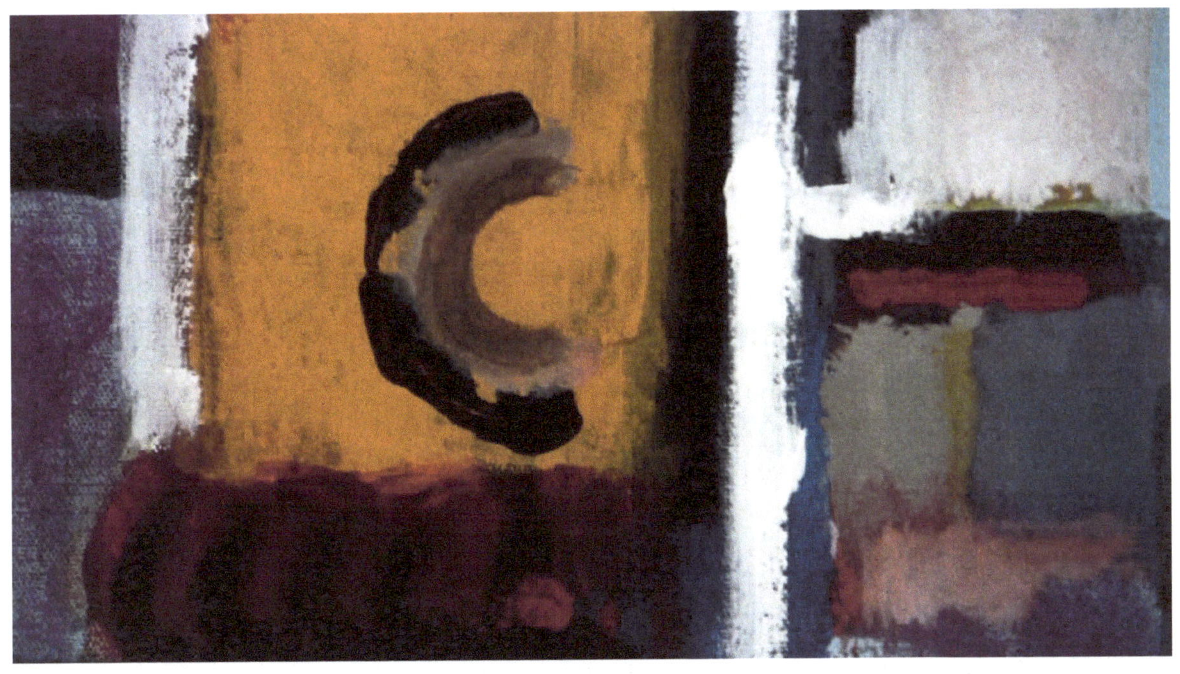

Details of "The Mustard Seed"

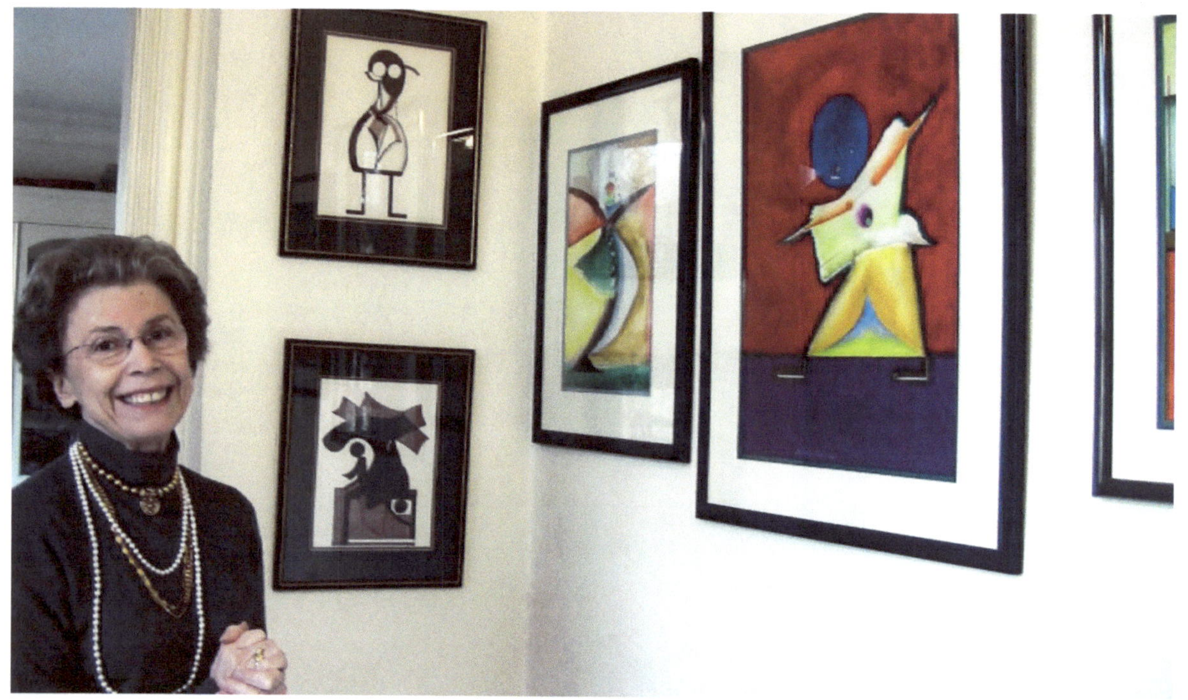

Isabel Taylor in her studio office, in front of works on paper by Eugene Martin

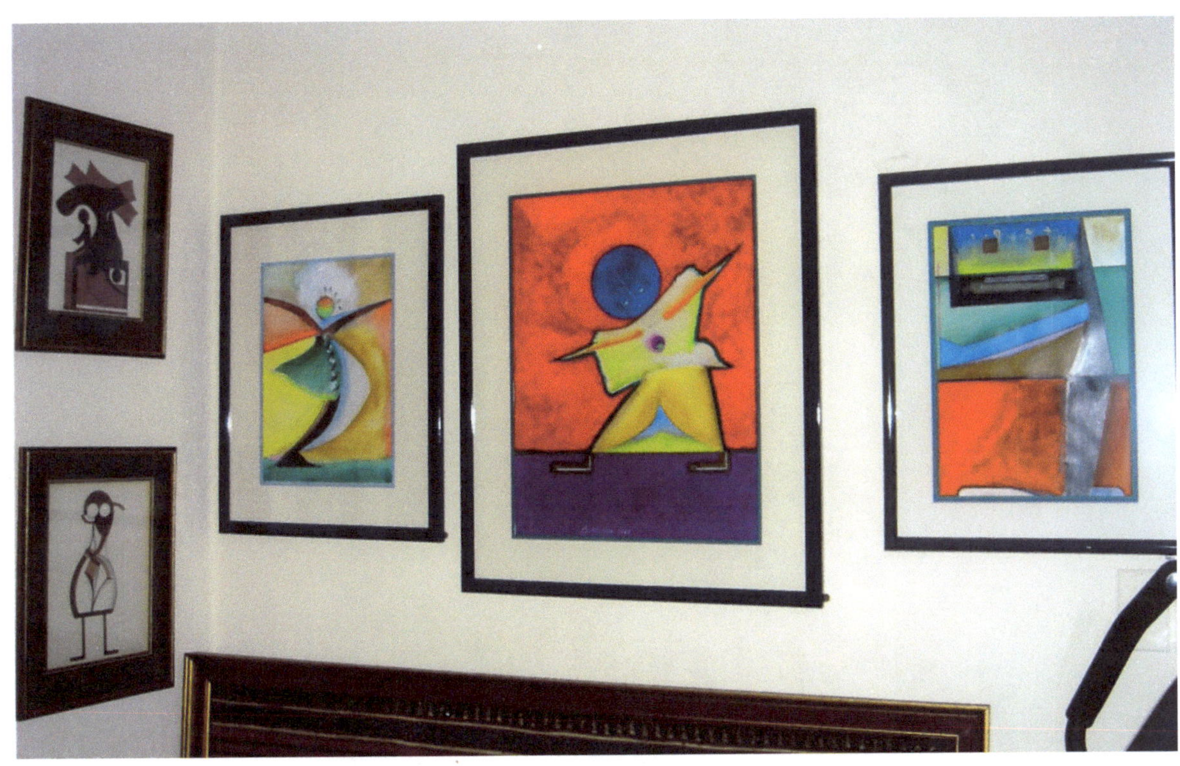

Works on paper by Eugene Martin in Isabel Taylor's studio office in Washington D.C.

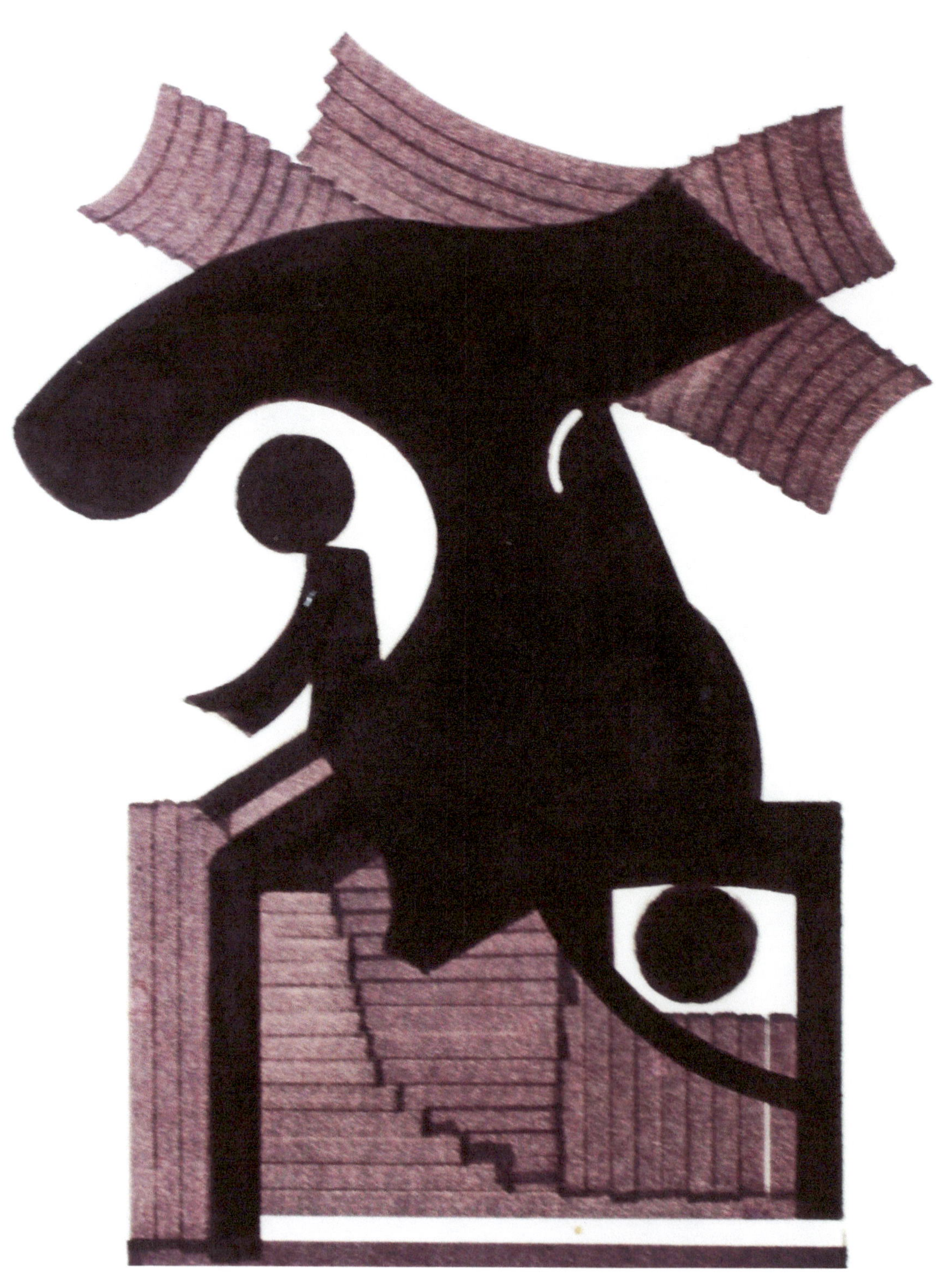

Ivory Child, felt-tip marker and pen & ink drawing by Eugene Martin, 1974

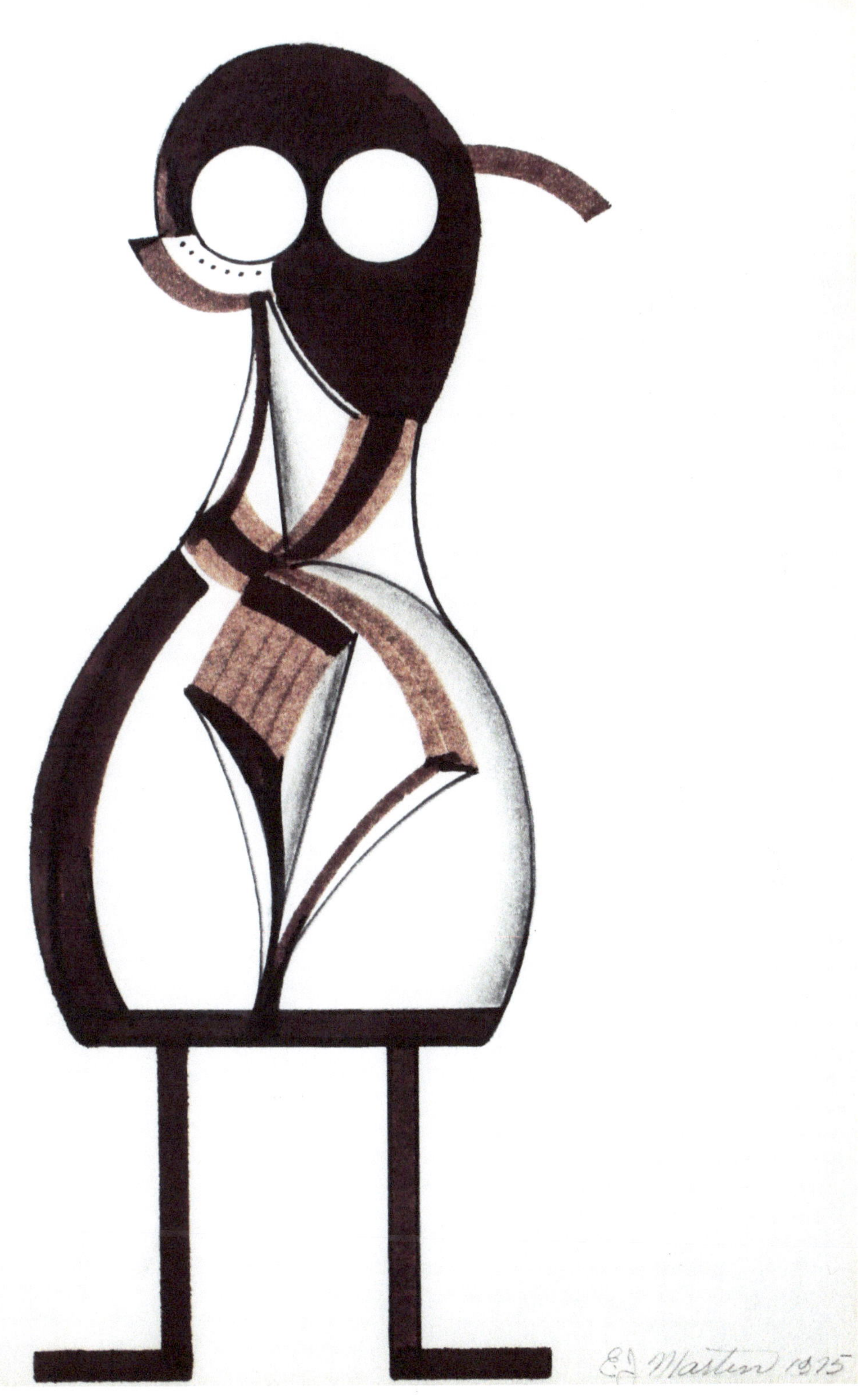

Handsome Myth, felt-tip marker, pen & ink and graphite drawing by Eugene Martin, 1975

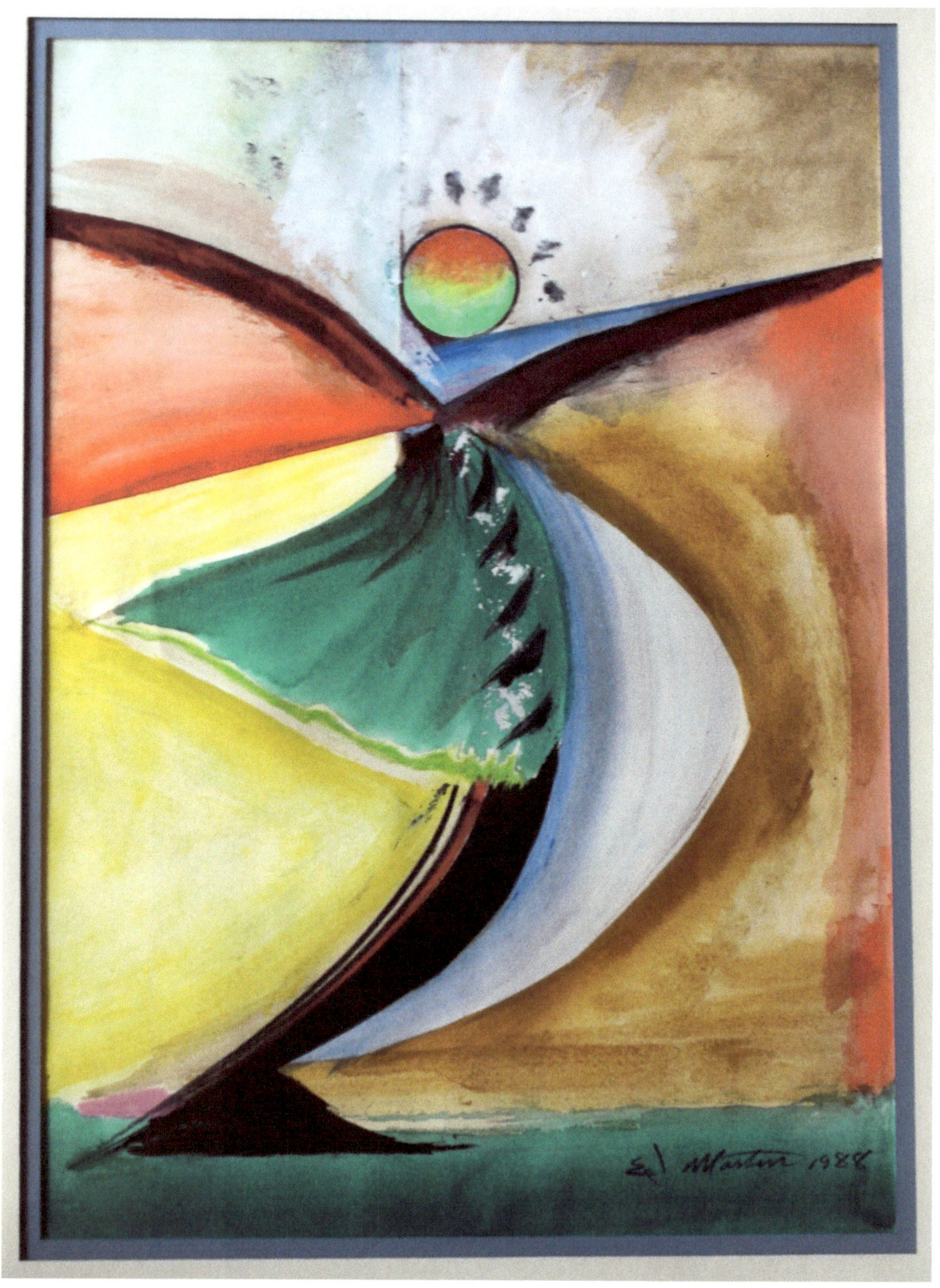

Untitled, 1988 acrylic painting on paper by Eugene Martin

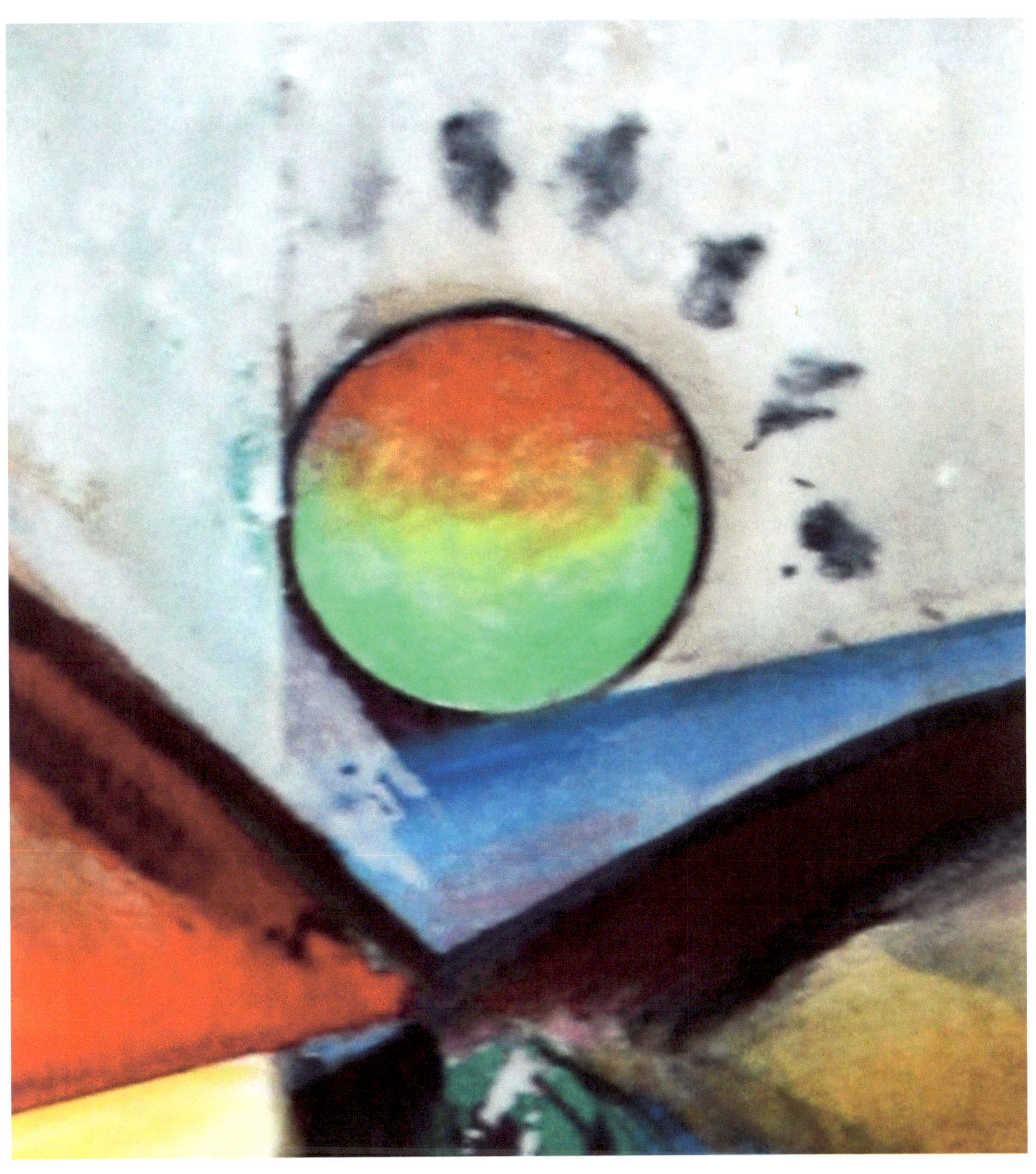

Detail of untitled 1988 acrylic painting on paper by Eugene Martin

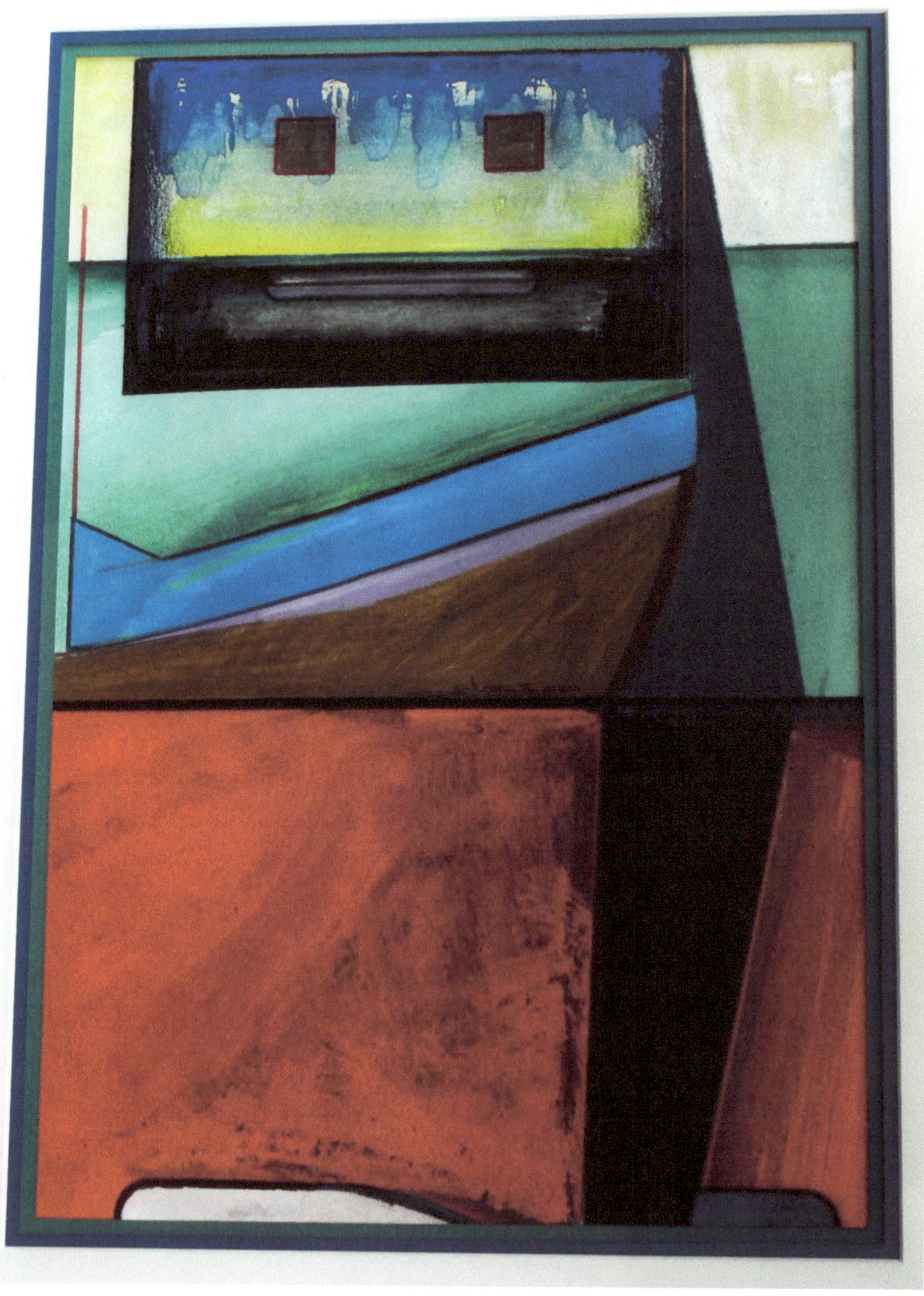

Untitled, 1989 acrylic painting on paper by Eugene Martin

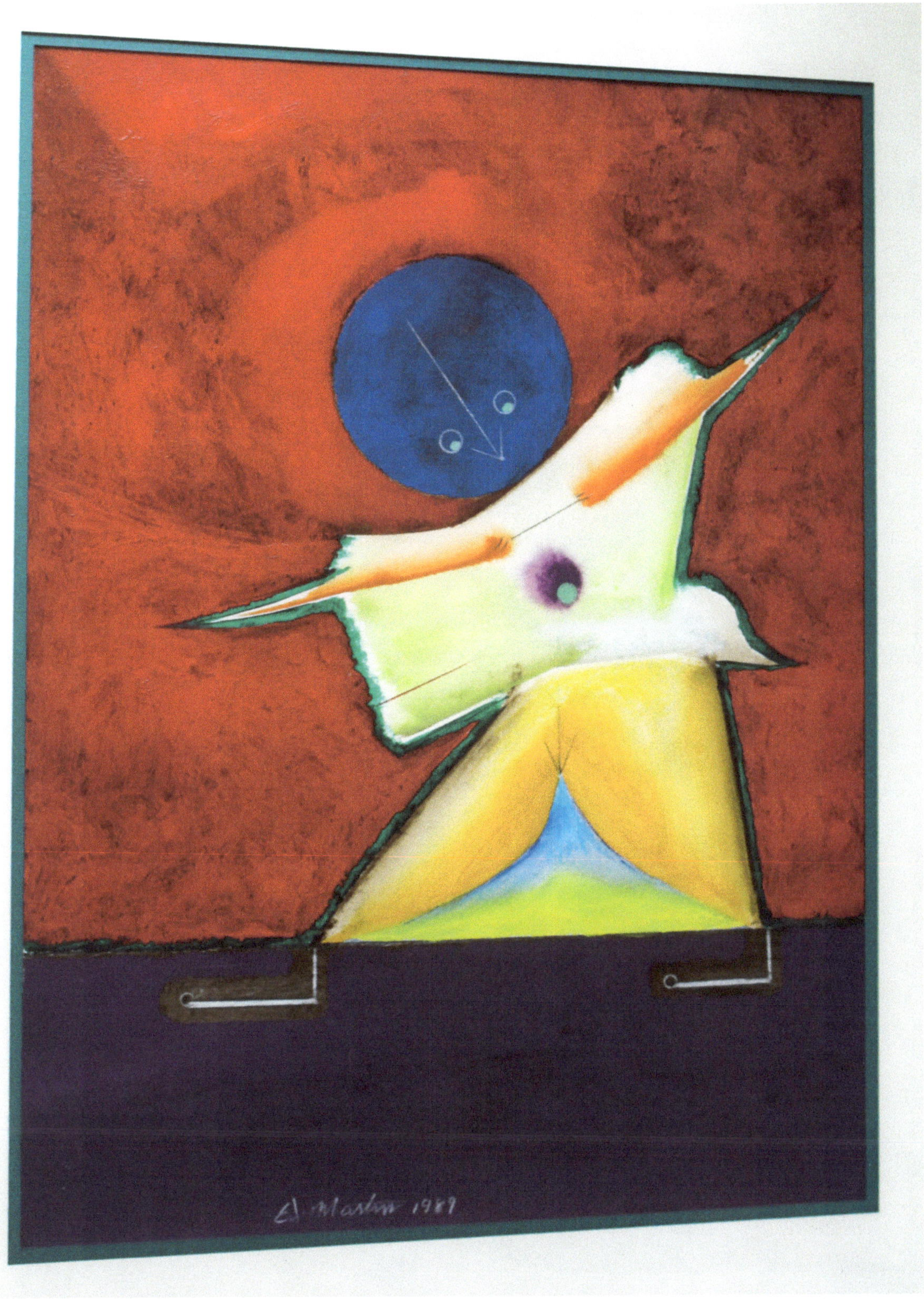

Untitled, 1989 acrylic painting on paper by Eugene Martin

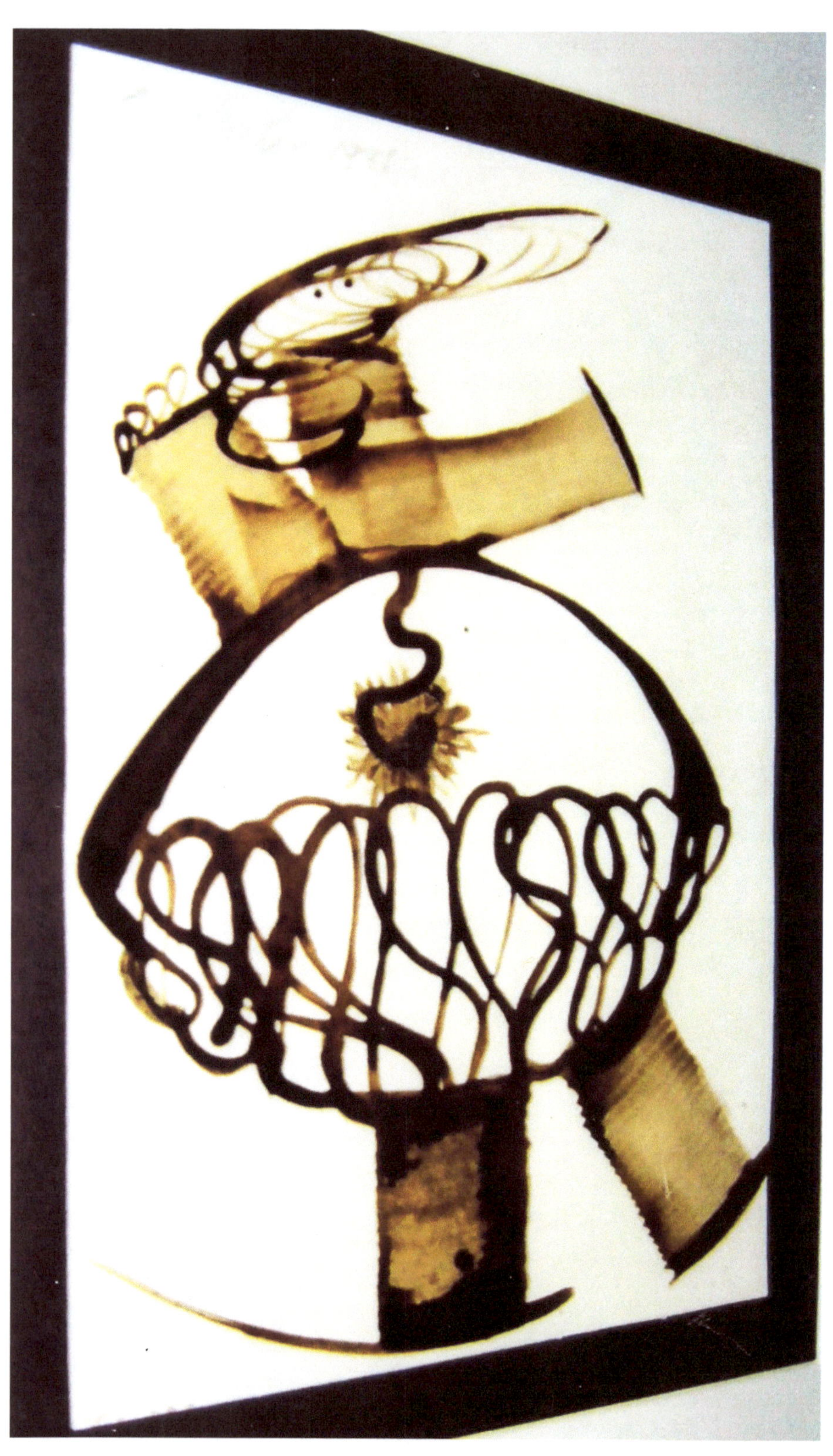

Untitled, 1981 bamboo reed pen and ink drawing by Eugene Martin

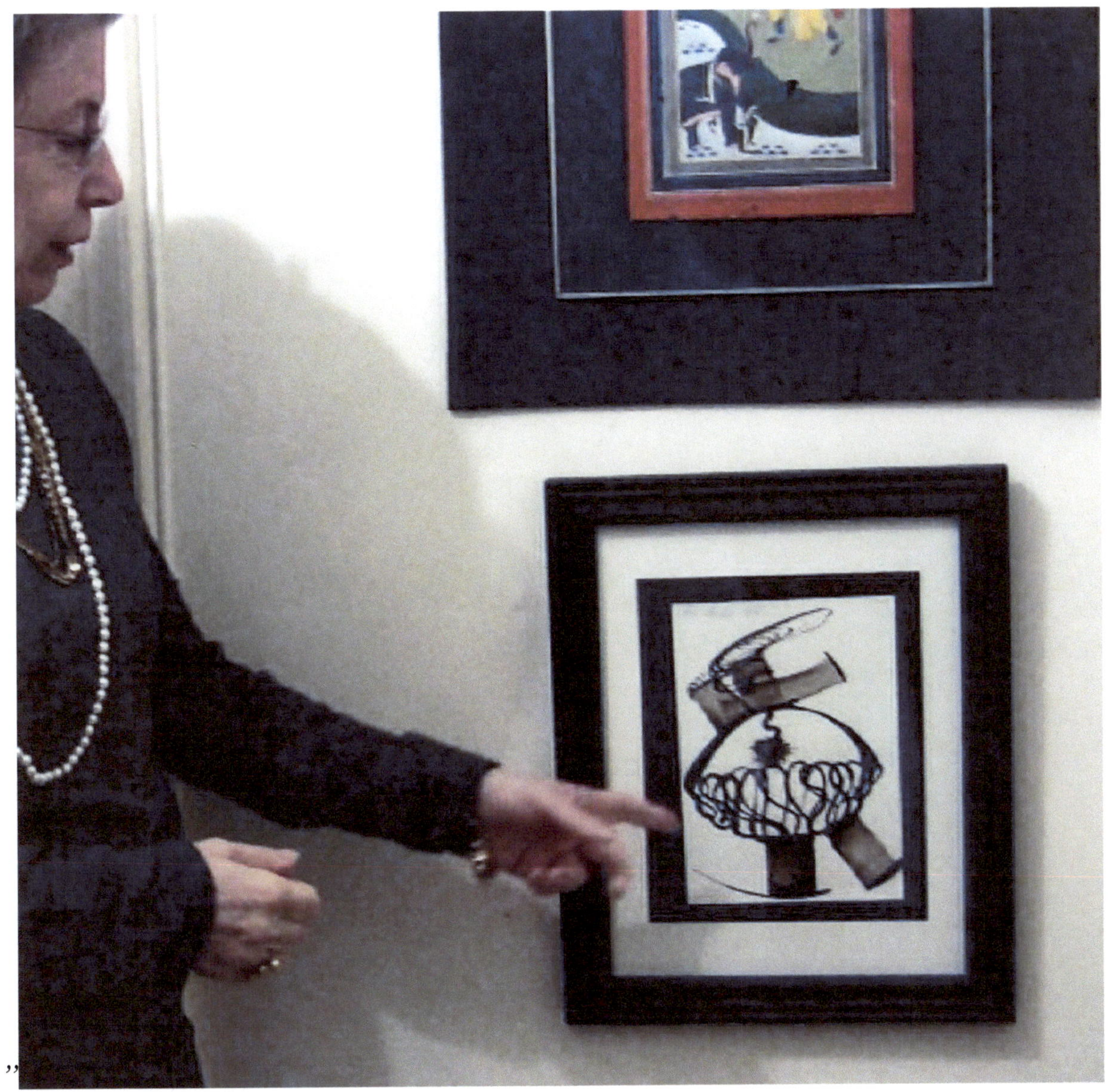

Isabel Taylor points toward her 1981 Eugene Martin bamboo reed pen and ink drawing

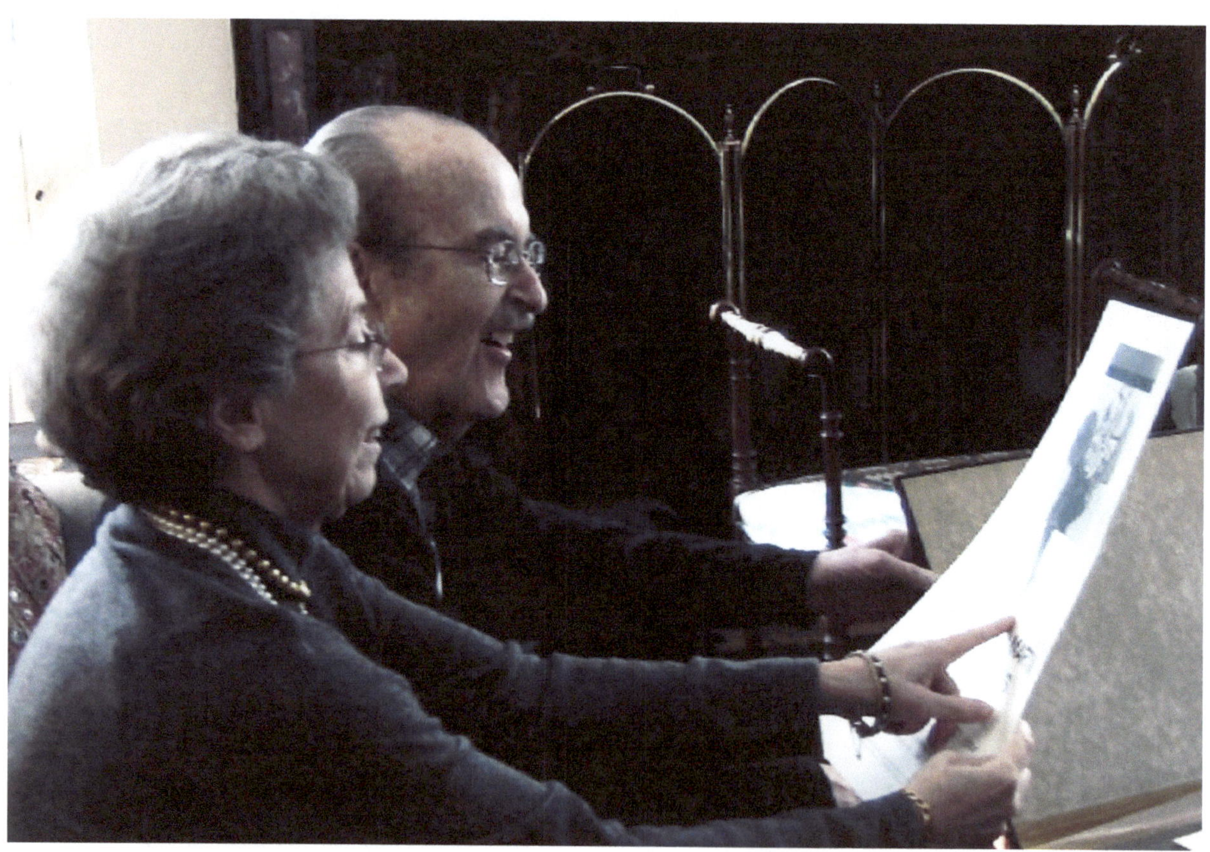

Isabel and David Taylor reminisce about Eugene Martin's 1994 exhibit at Duke University in their living room in Washington D.C.

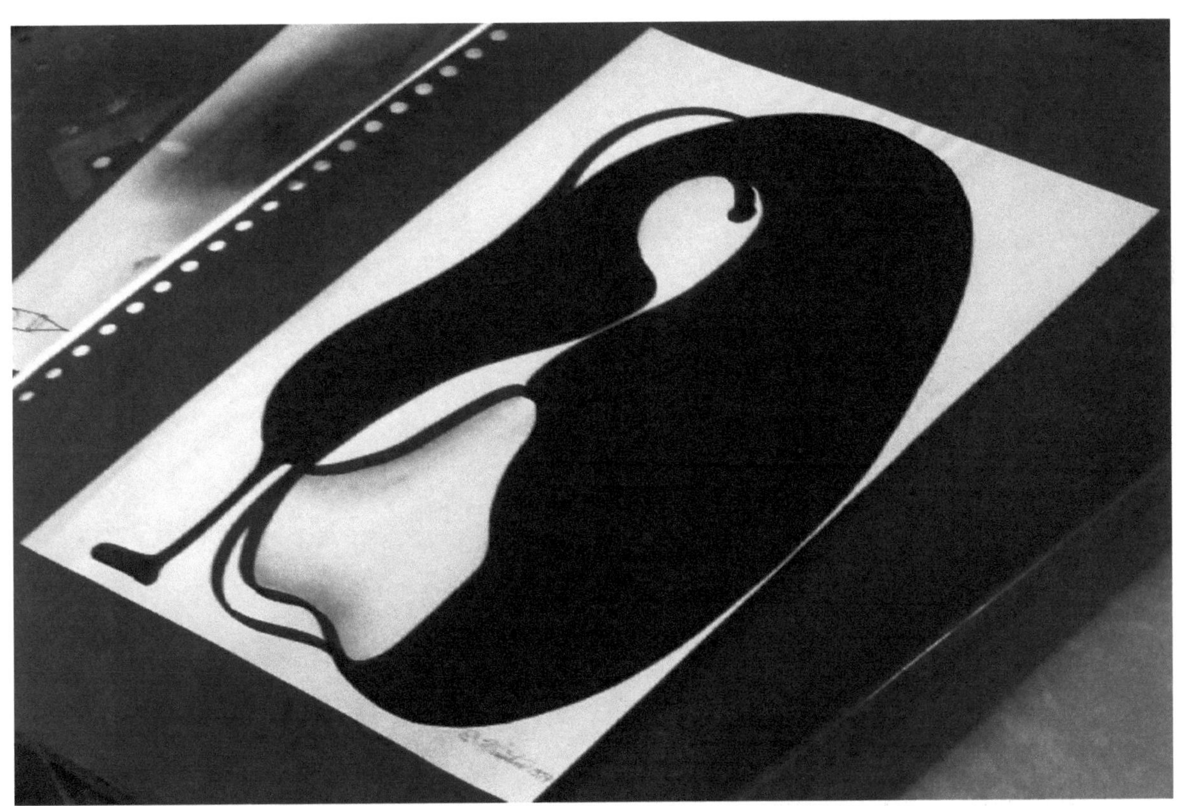

Untitled, 1979 pen and ink and graphite drawing by Eugene Martin

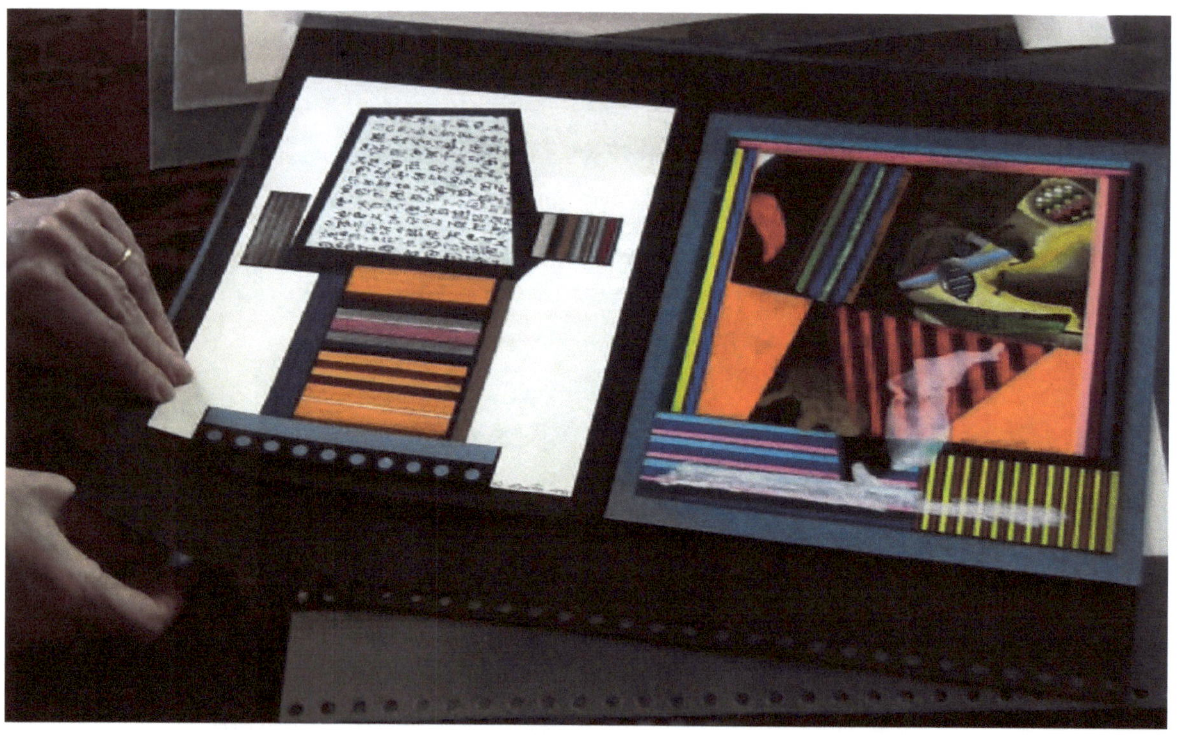

Untitled, 1980 mixed media works on paper, collage, by Eugene Martin

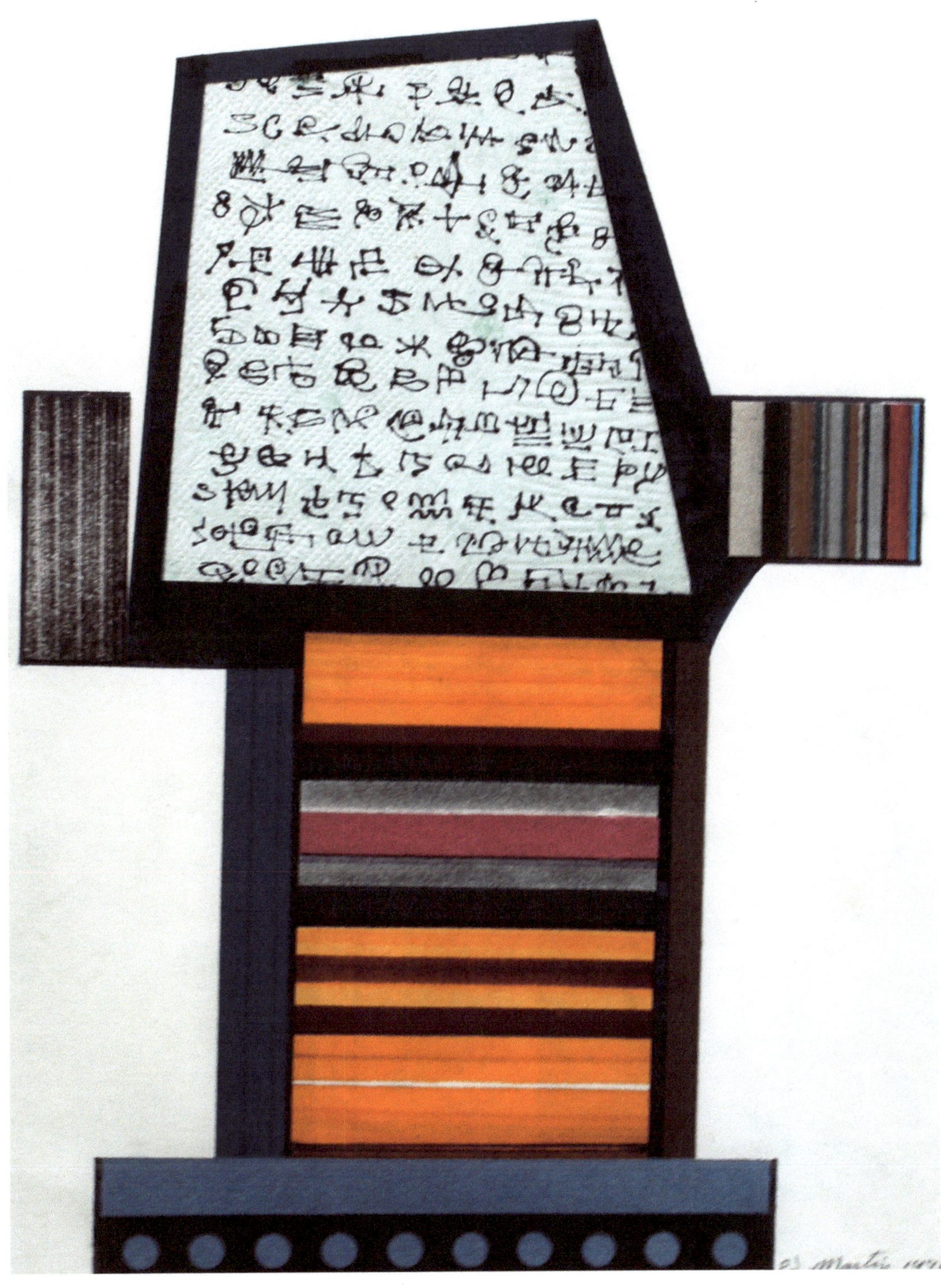

Untitled, 1980 mixed media work on paper, collage, by Eugene Martin

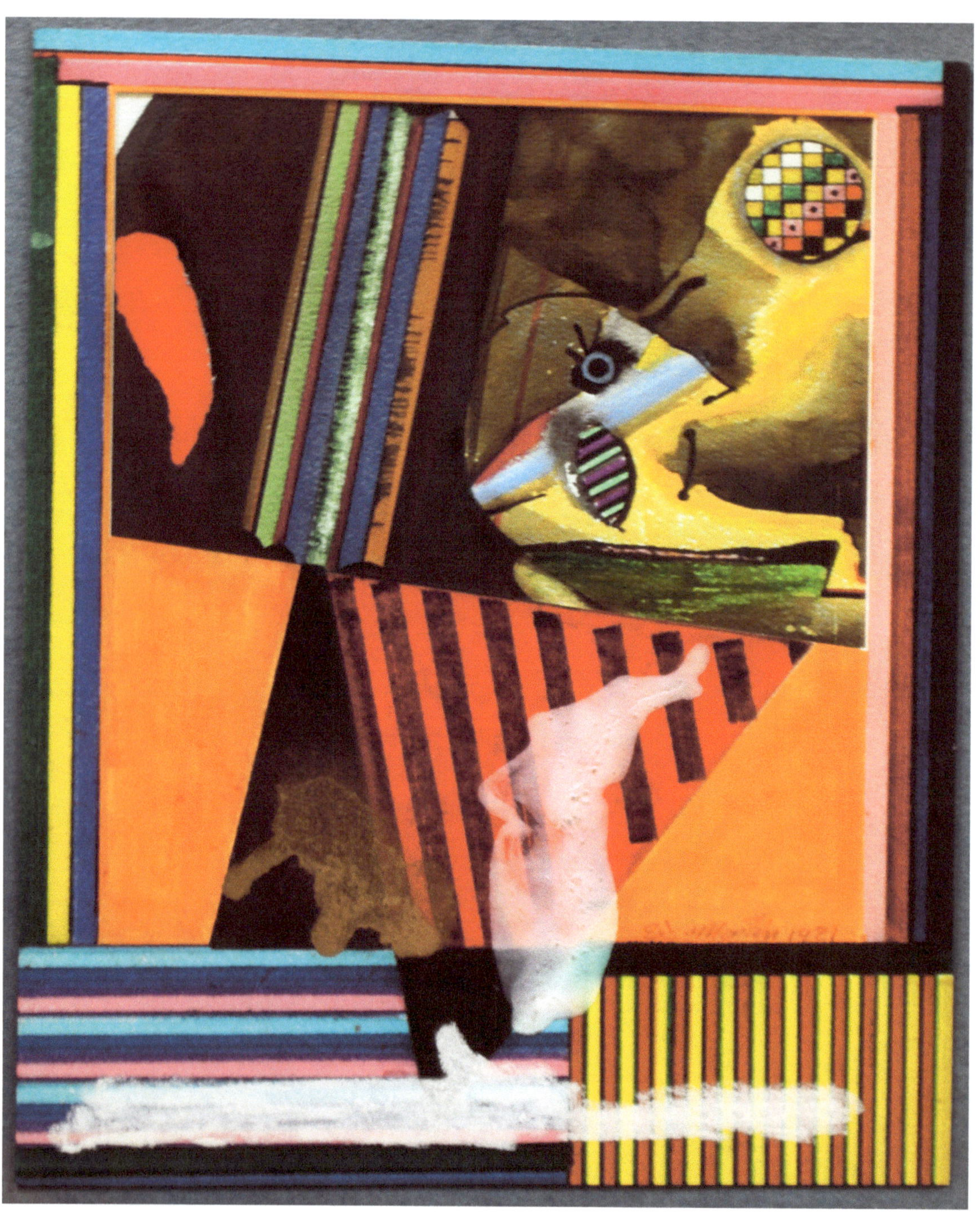

Untitled, 1980 mixed media work on paper by Eugene Martin

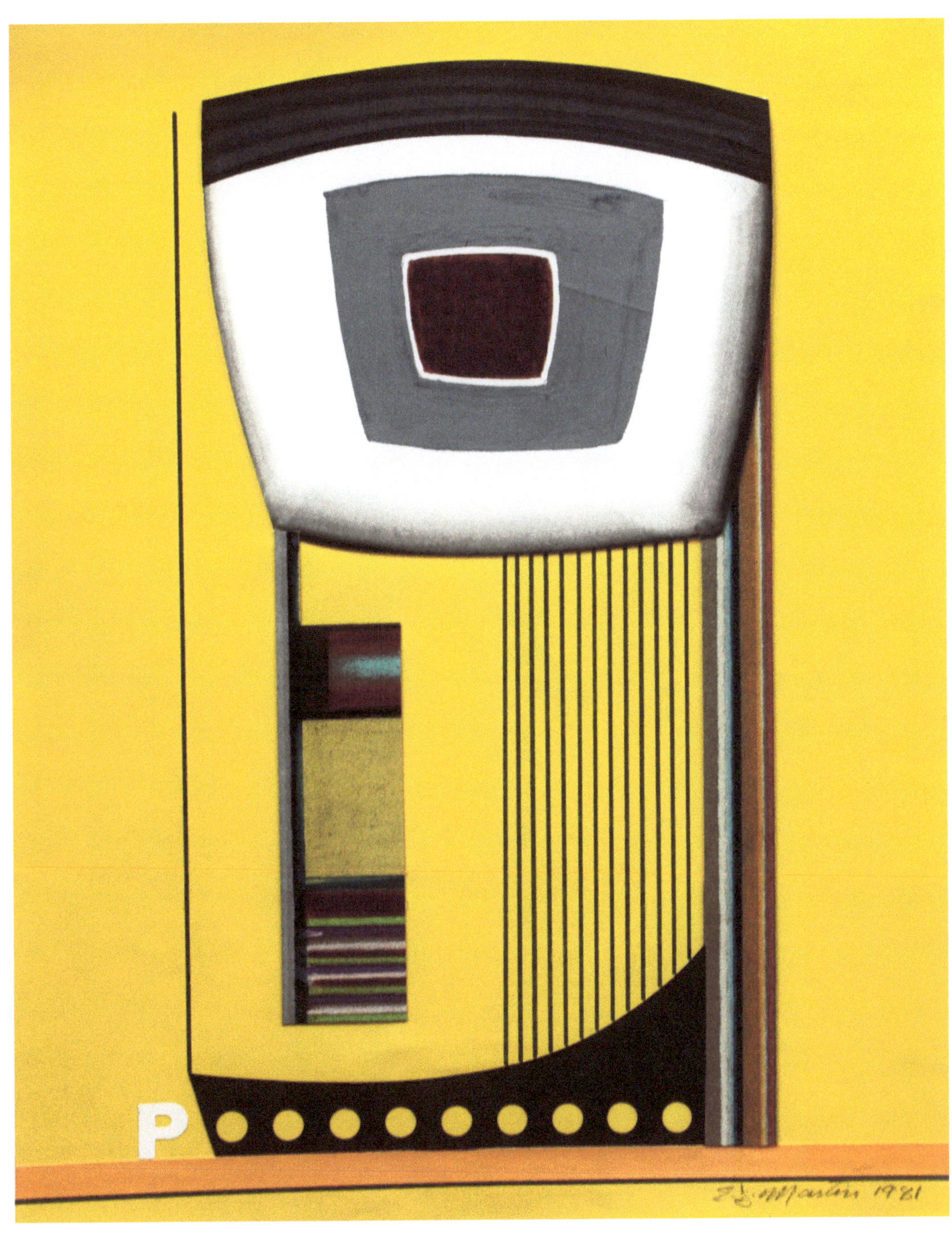

Untitled, 1981 mixed media work on paper, collage, by Eugene Martin

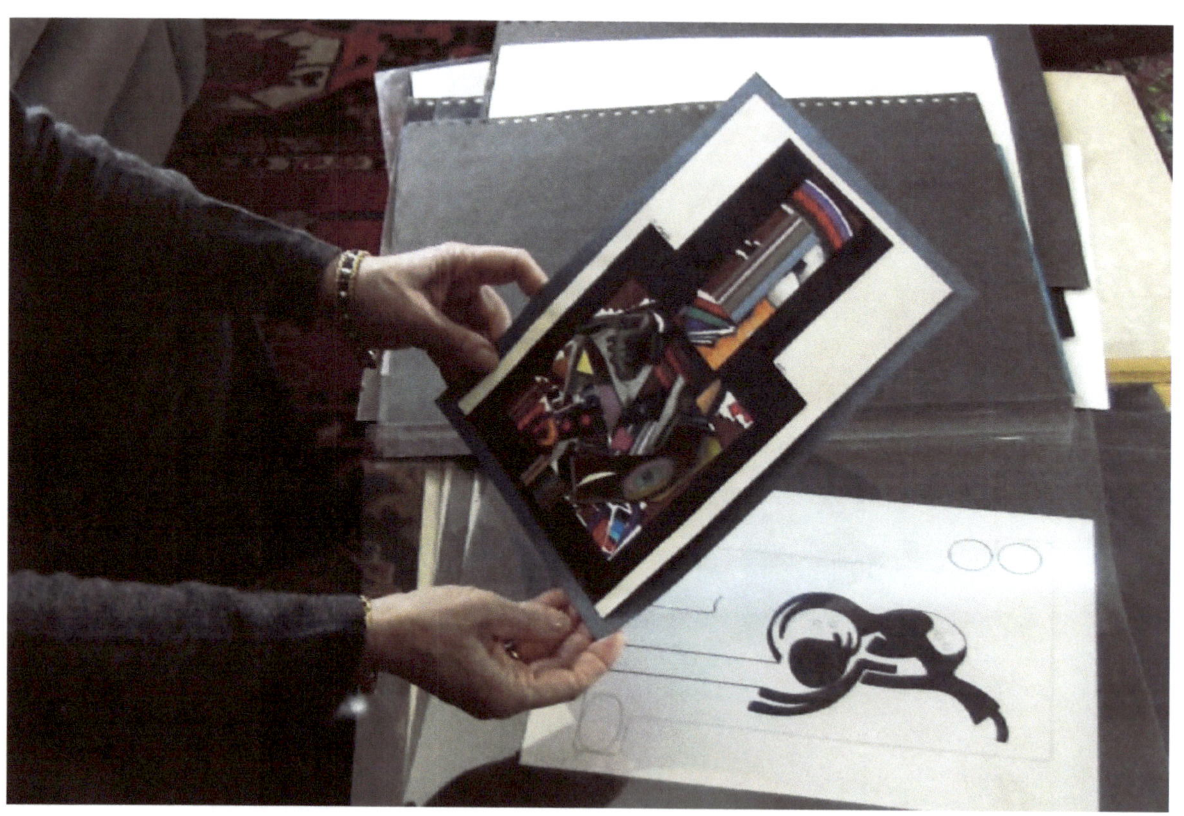

Untitled, 1980 mixed media work on paper by Eugene Martin

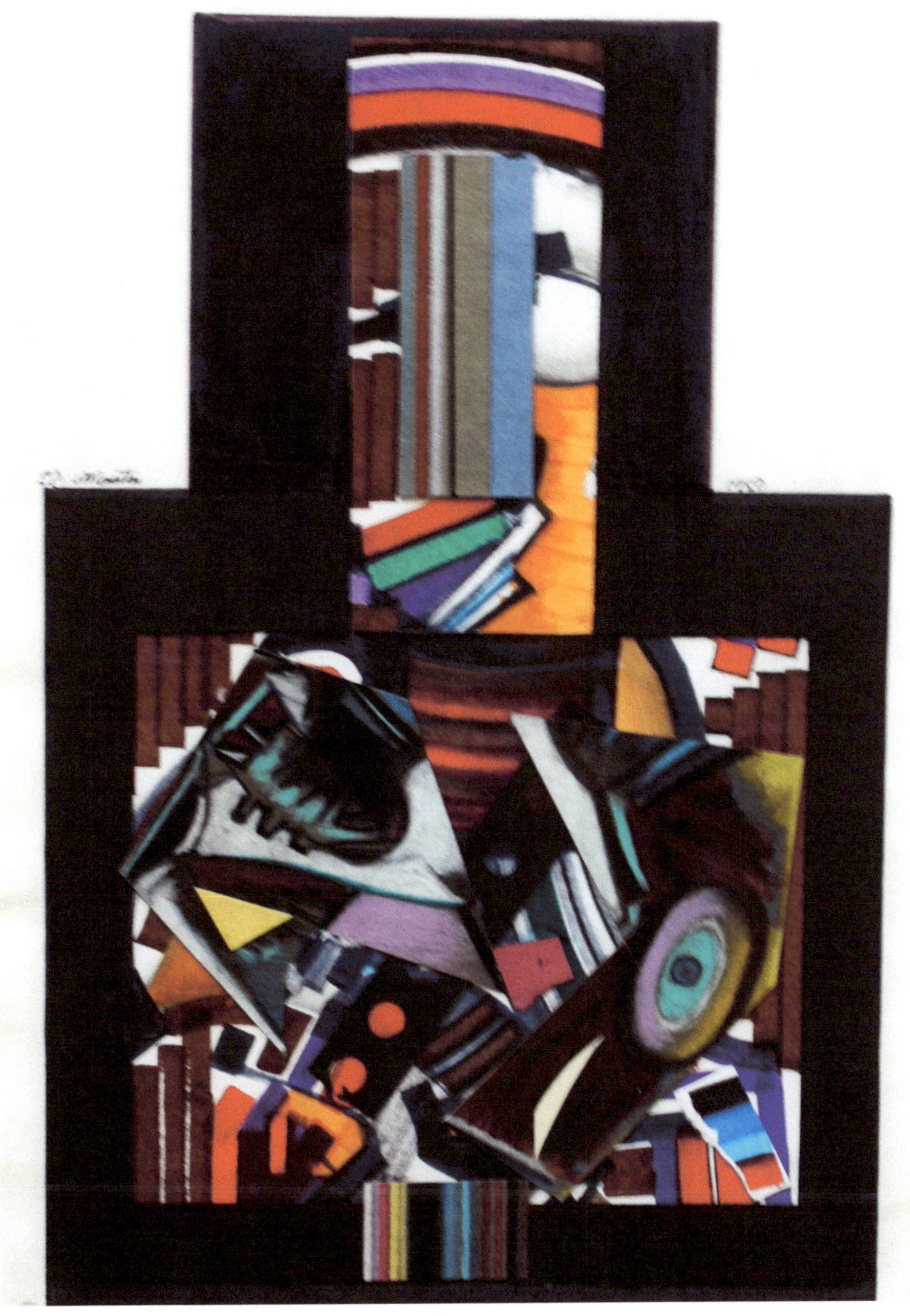

Untitled, 1980 mixed work on paper by Eugene Martin

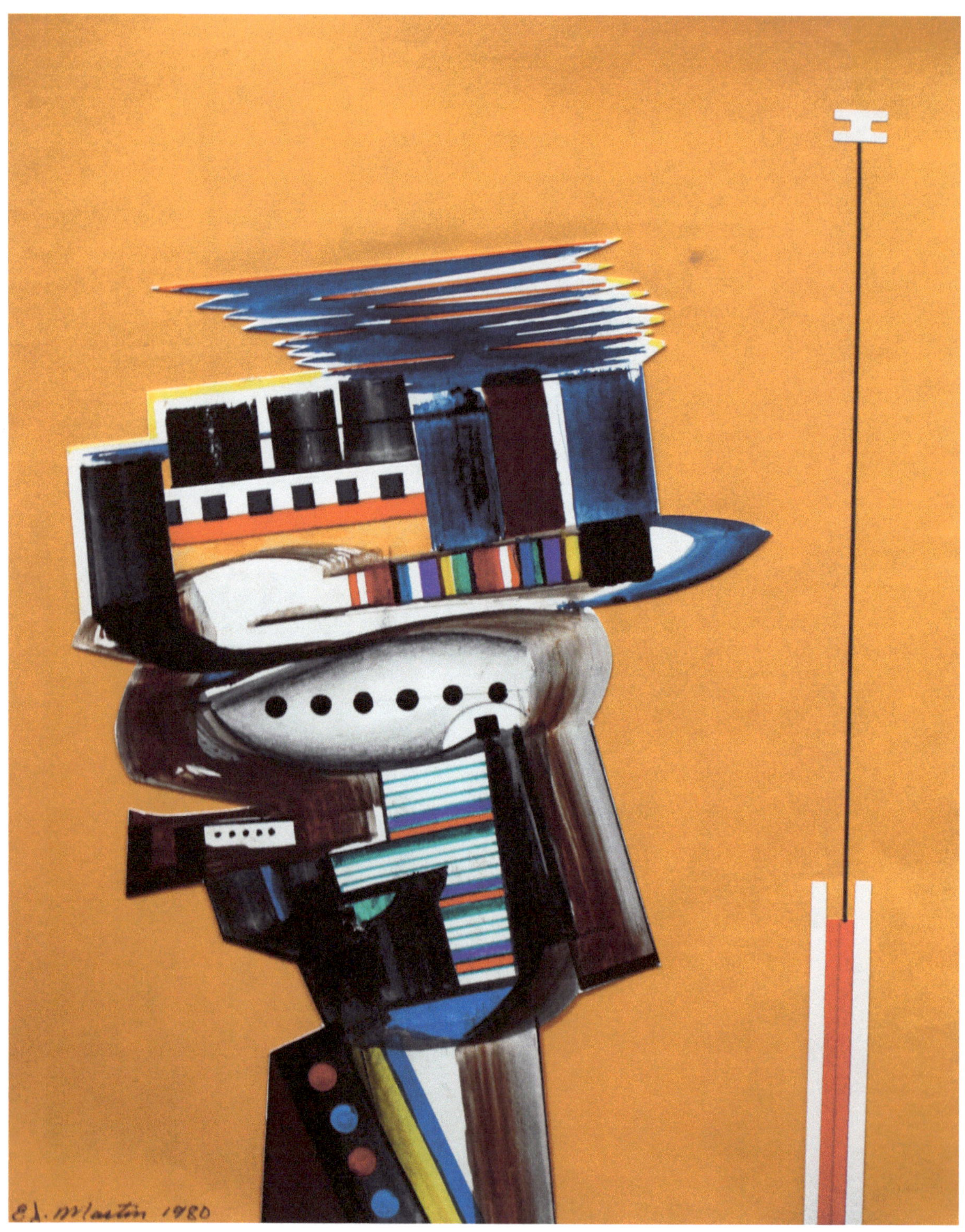

Untitled, 1980 mixed work on paper by Eugene Martin

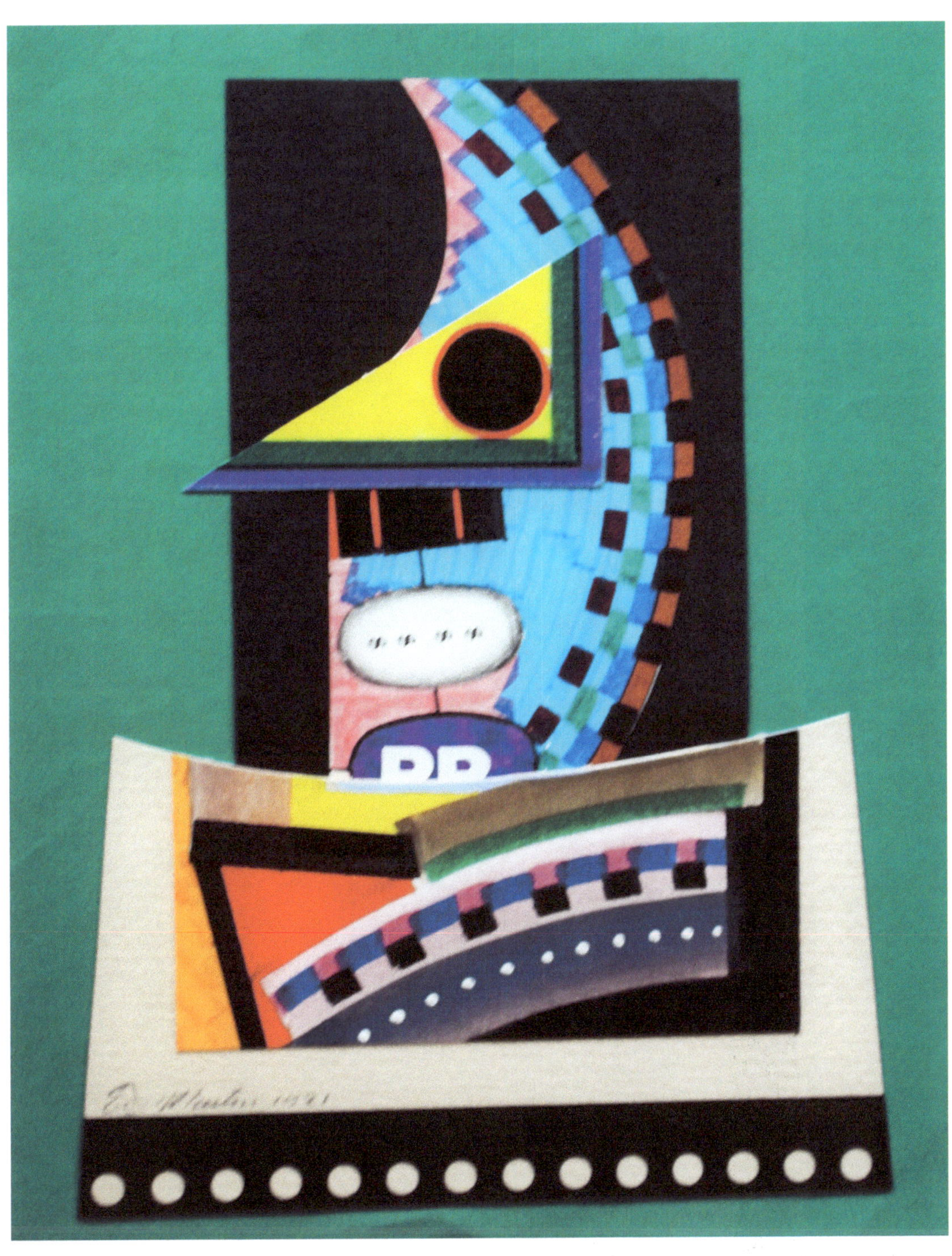

Untitled, 1981 mixed work on paper, collage, by Eugene Martin

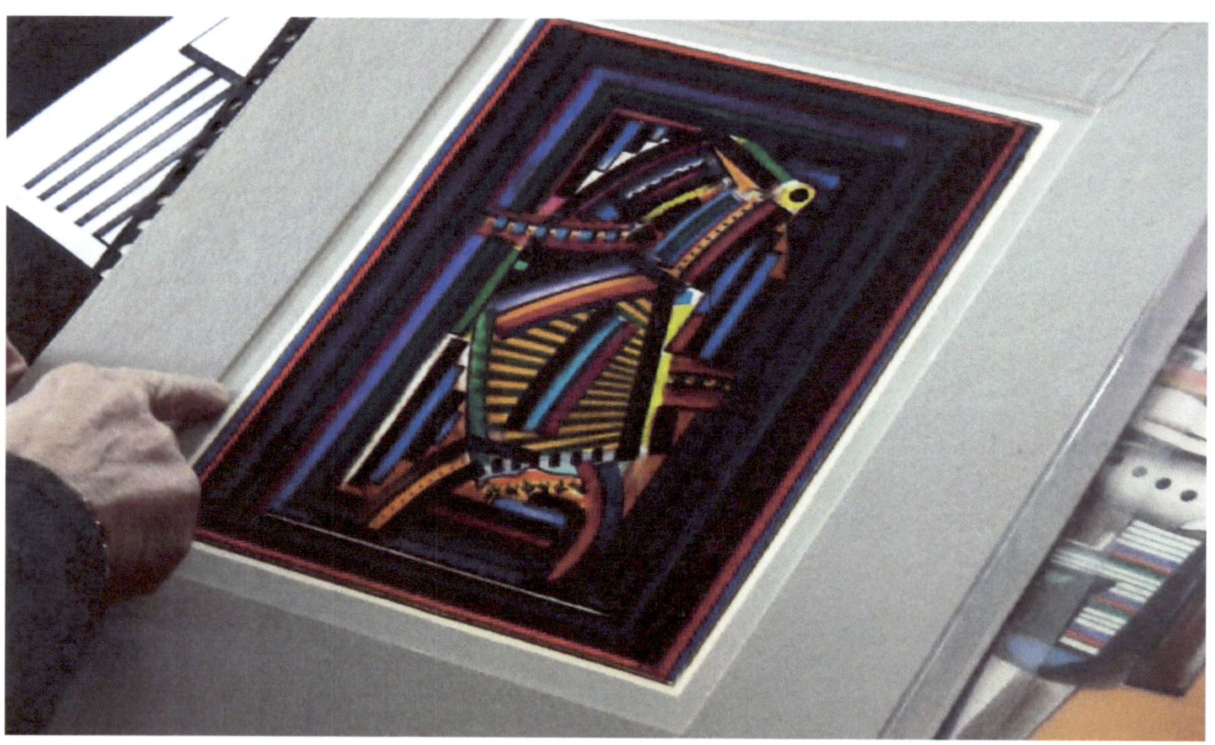

Untitled, 1980 felt-tip marker on paper by Eugene Martin

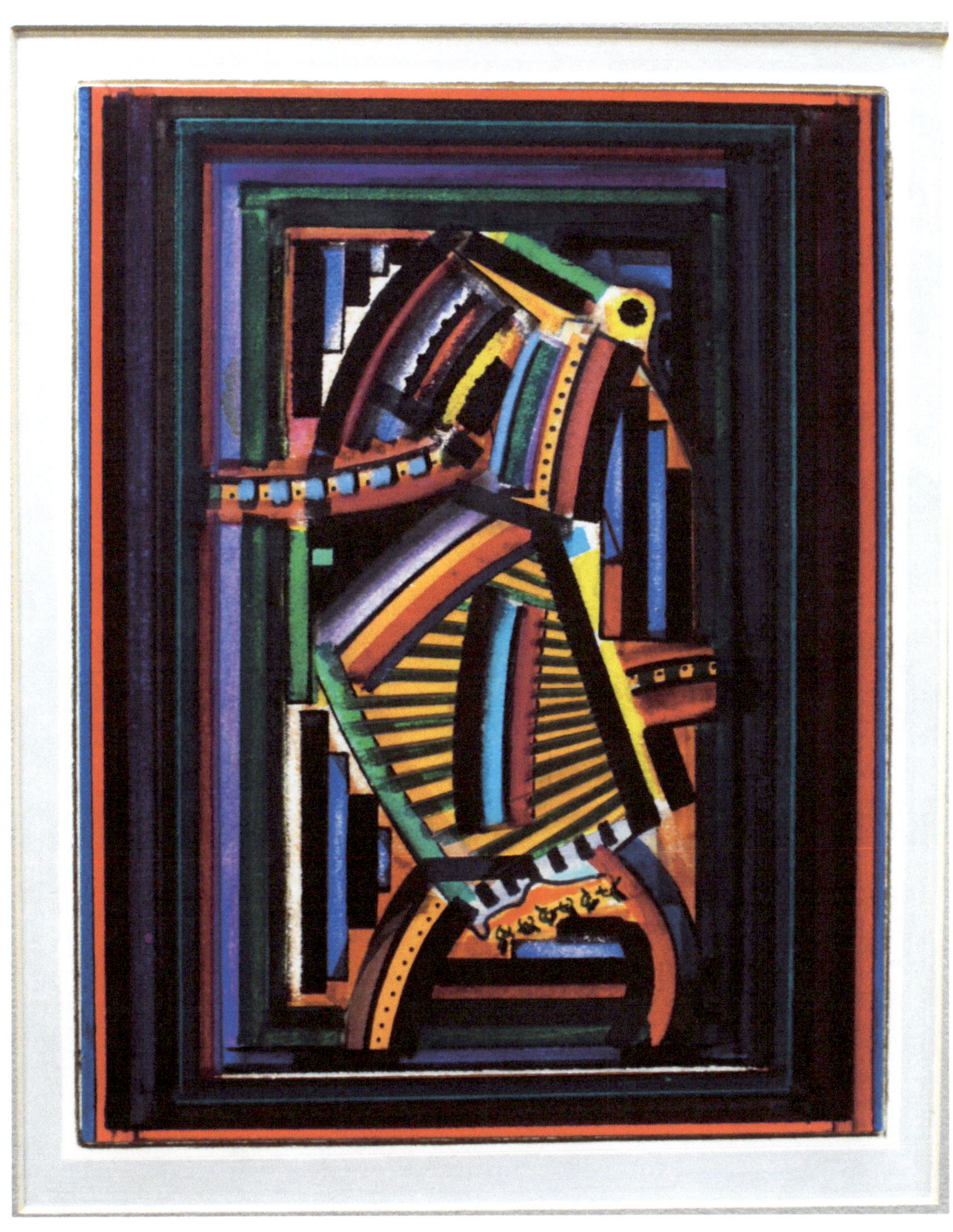

Untitled, 1980 felt-tip marker on paper by Eugene Martin

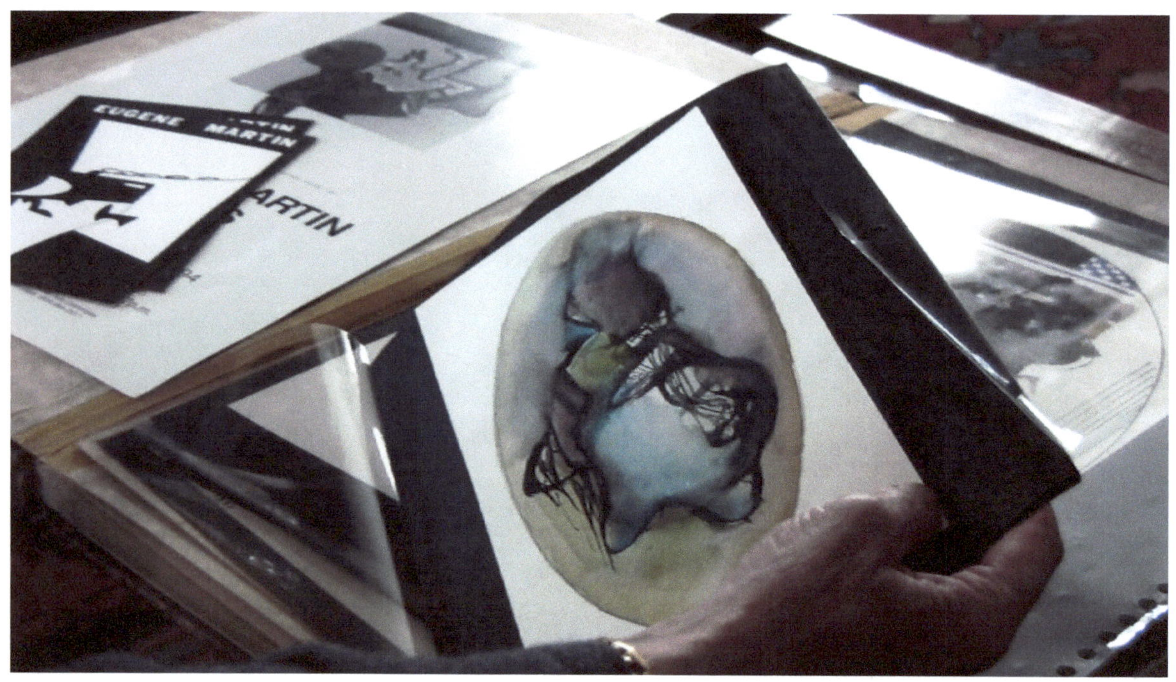

Untitled, 1970 watercolor drawing by Eugene Martin

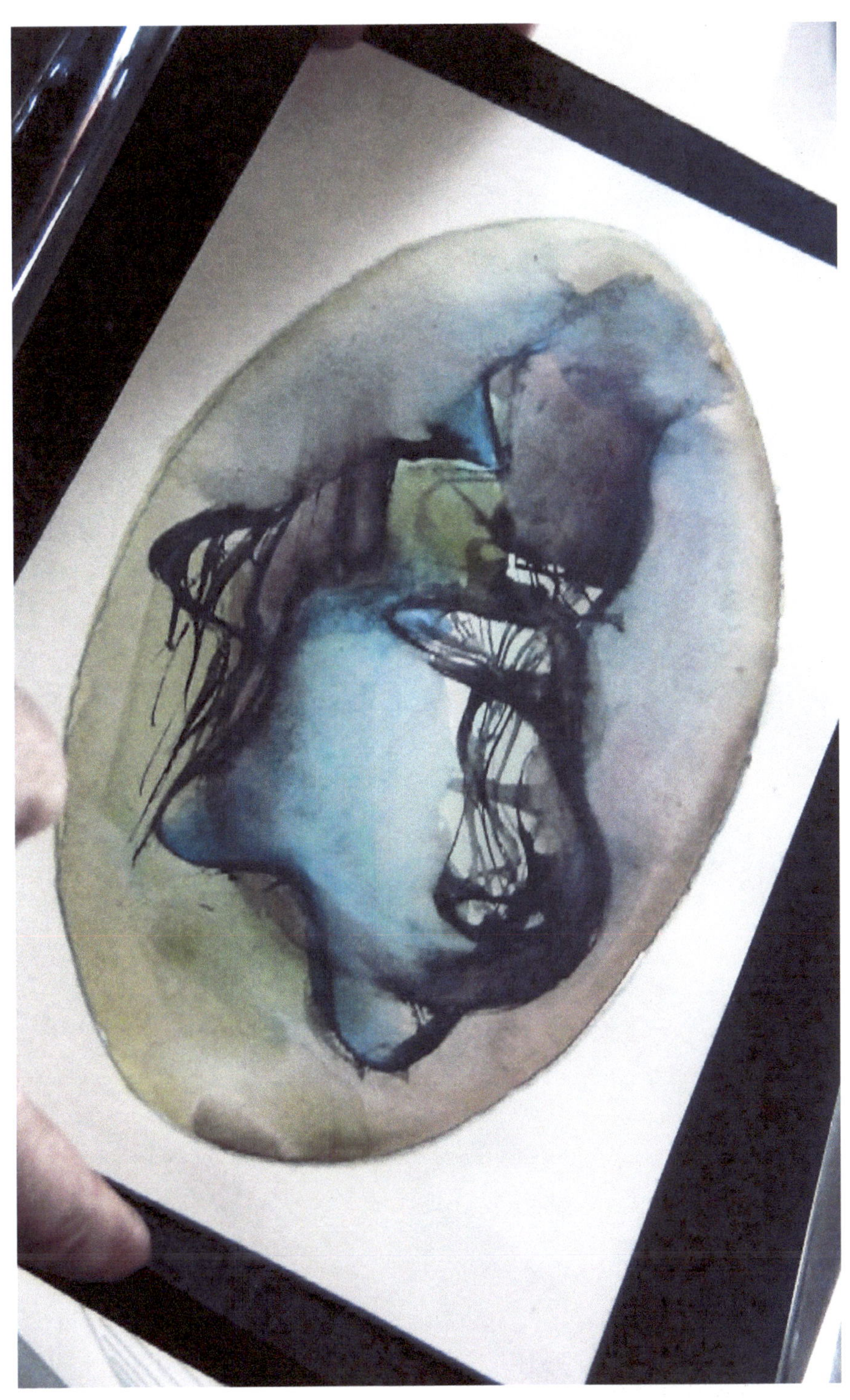

Untitled, 1970 watercolor drawing by Eugene Martin

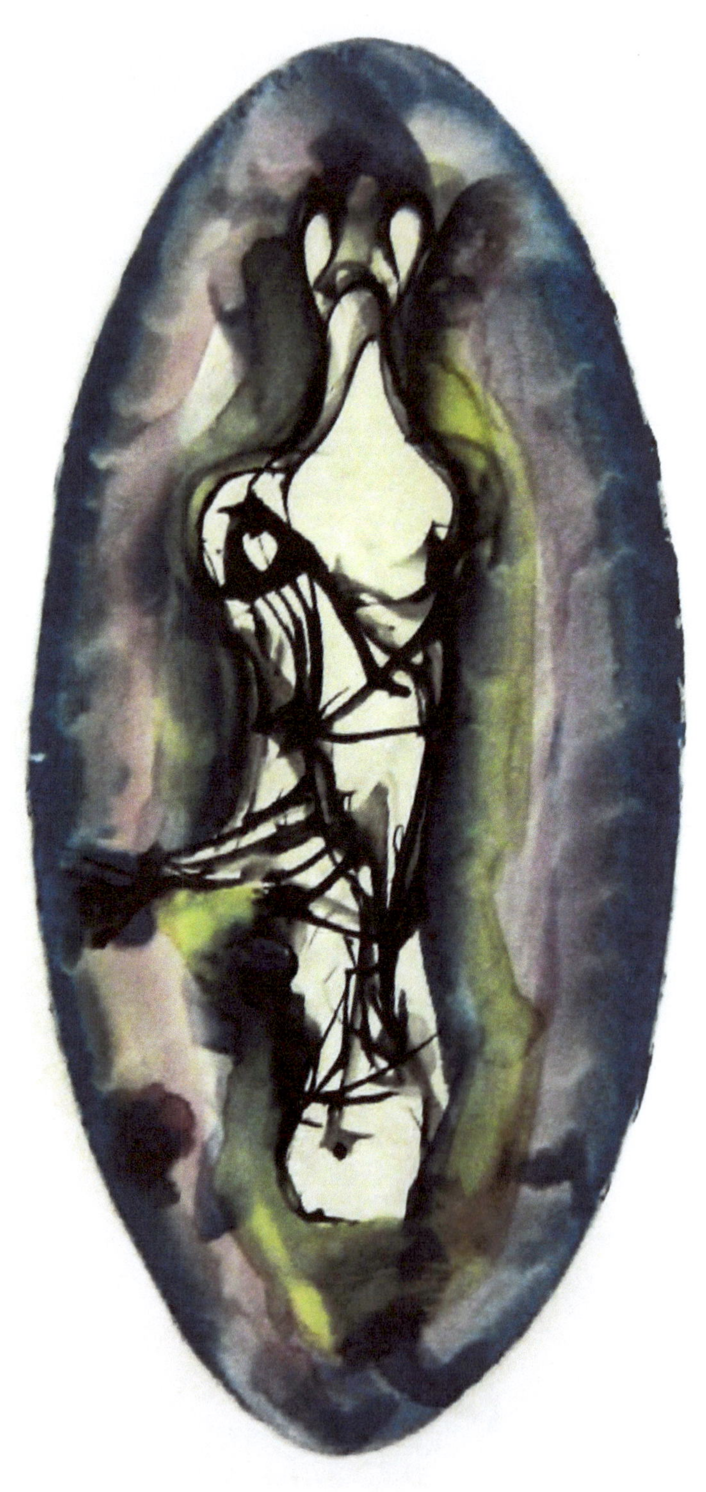

Untitled, watercolor drawing by Eugene Martin, 1970

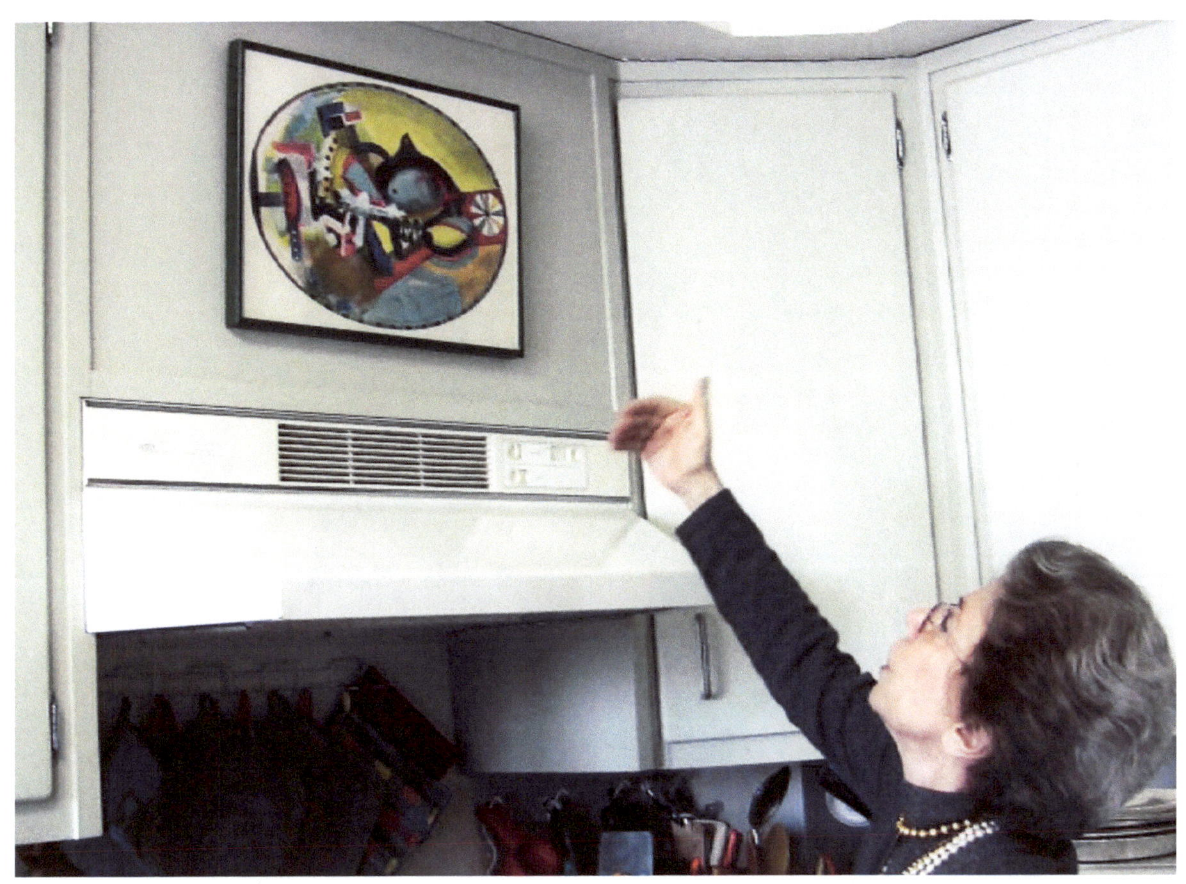

Isabel Taylor points to an untitled, 1973 mixed media oval drawing by Eugene Martin

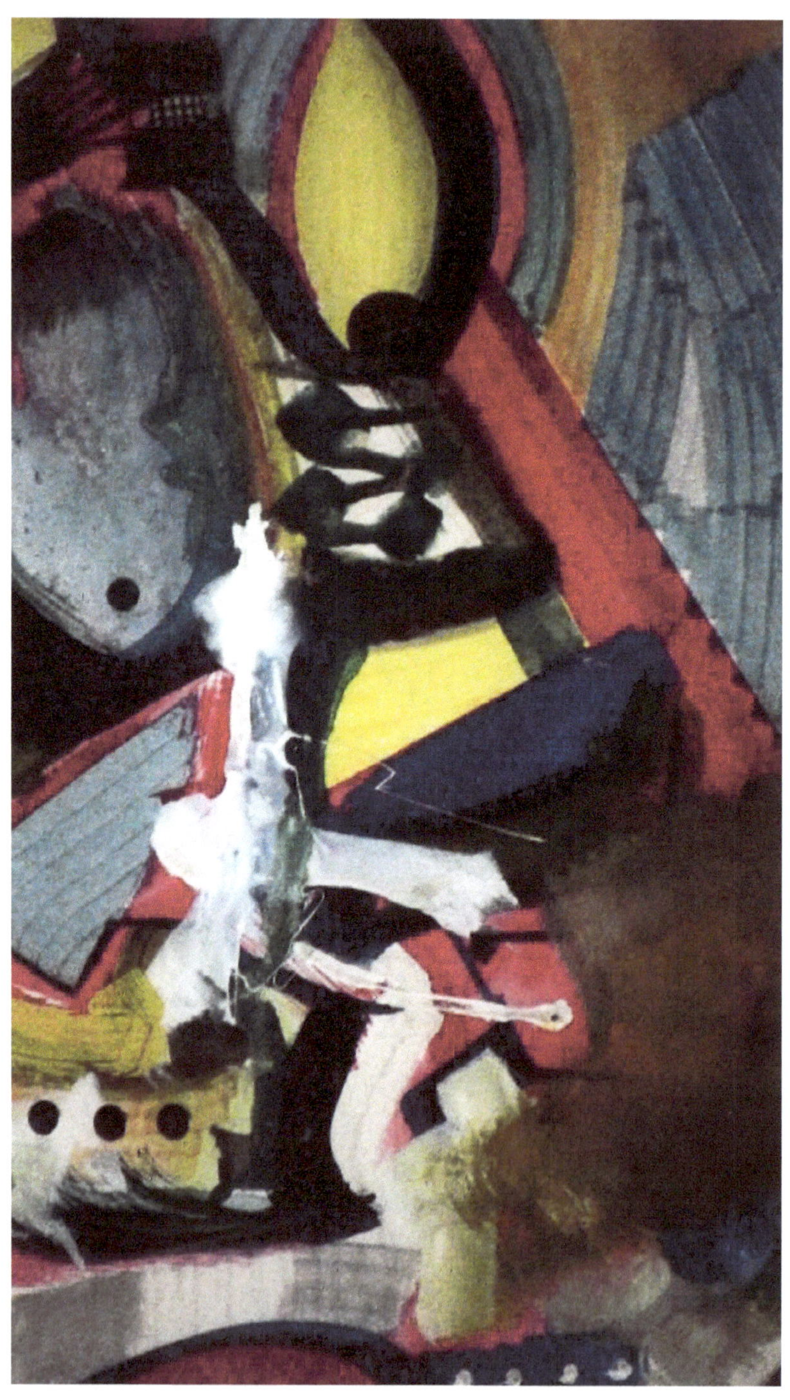

Detail of an untitled, 1973 mixed media oval drawing by Eugene Martin hanging in Isabel Taylor's kitchen in Washington D.C.

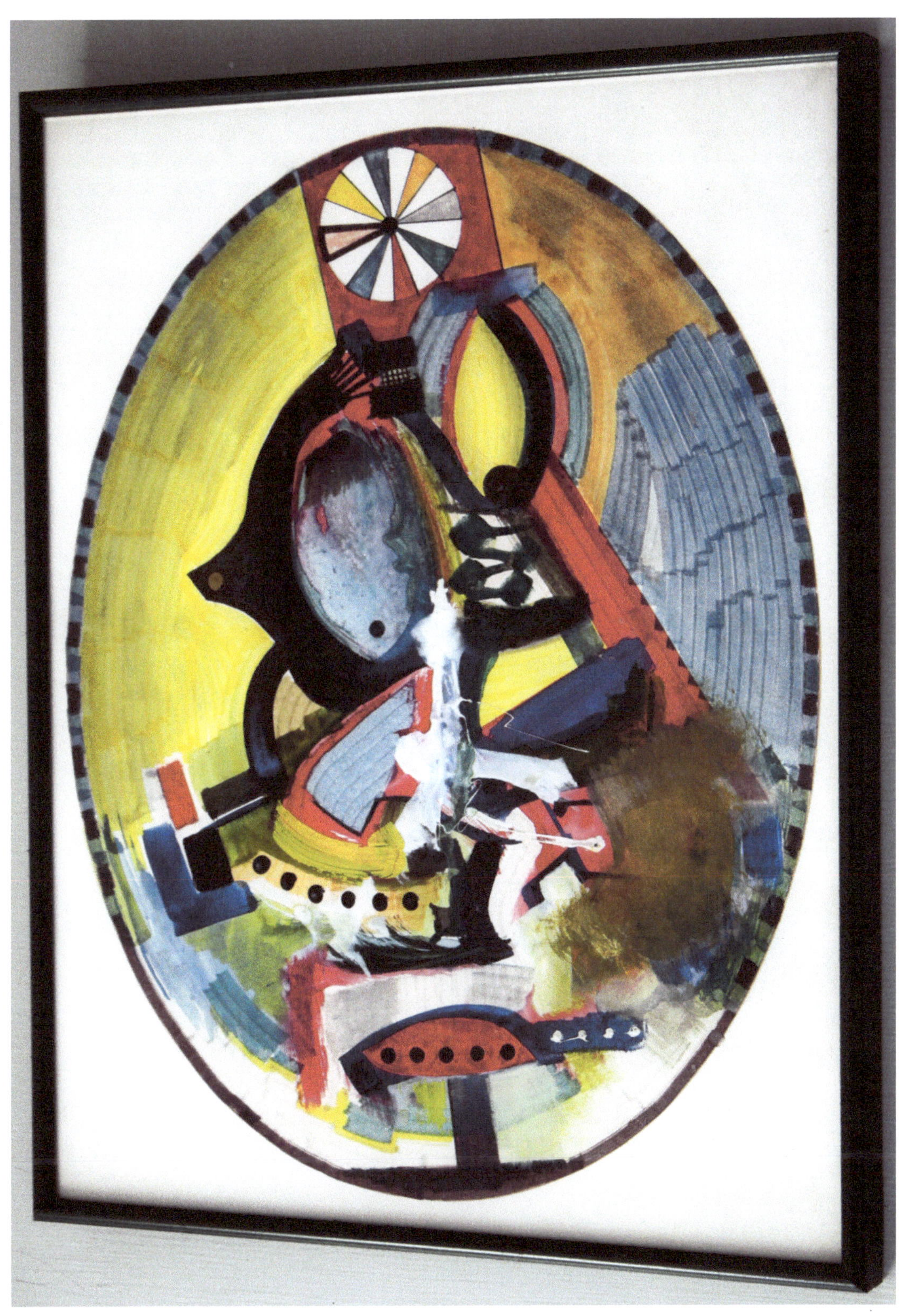

Untitled, 1973 mixed media oval drawing by Eugene Martin

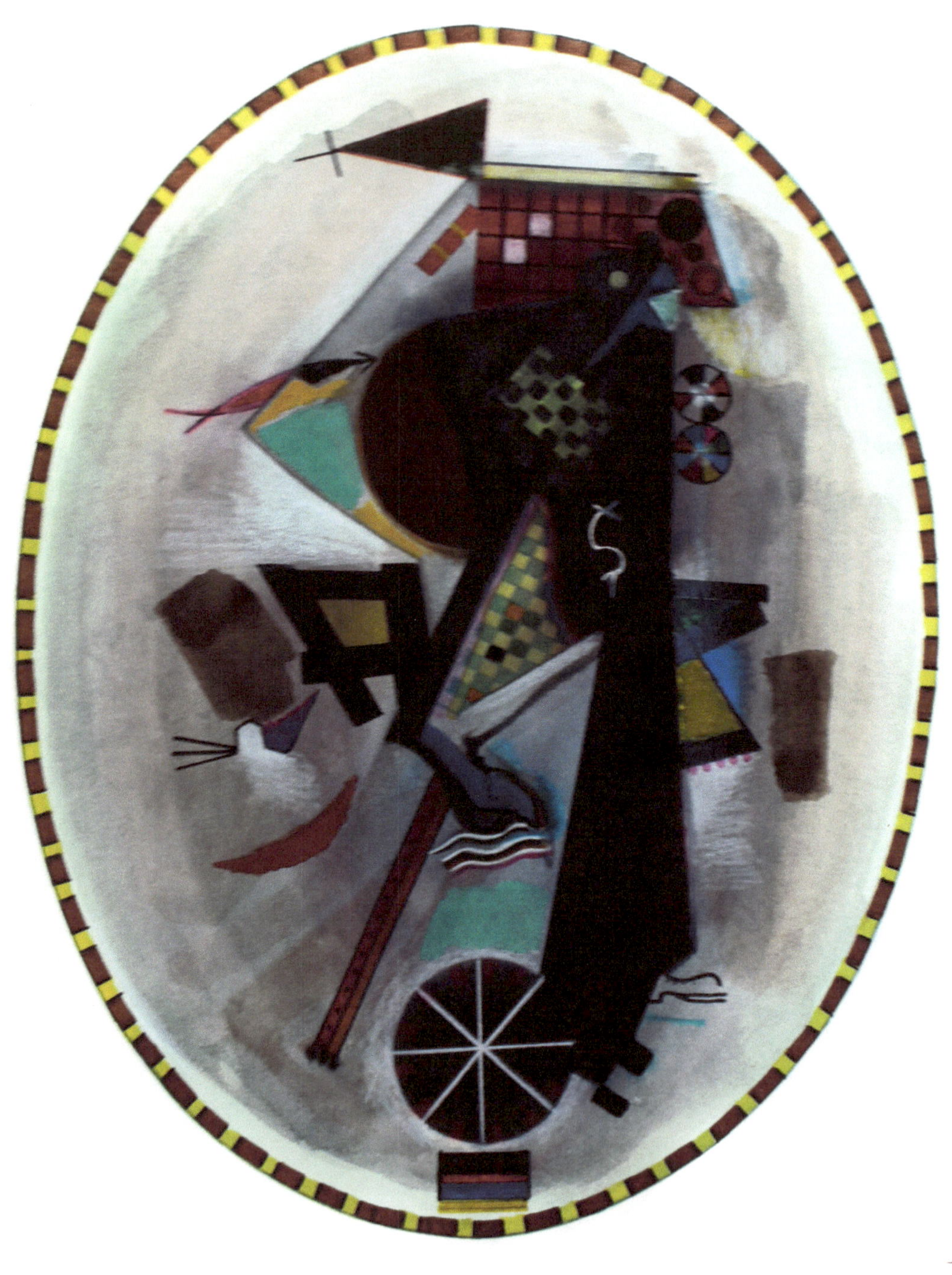

Untitled, 1972 mixed media oval drawing by Eugene Martin

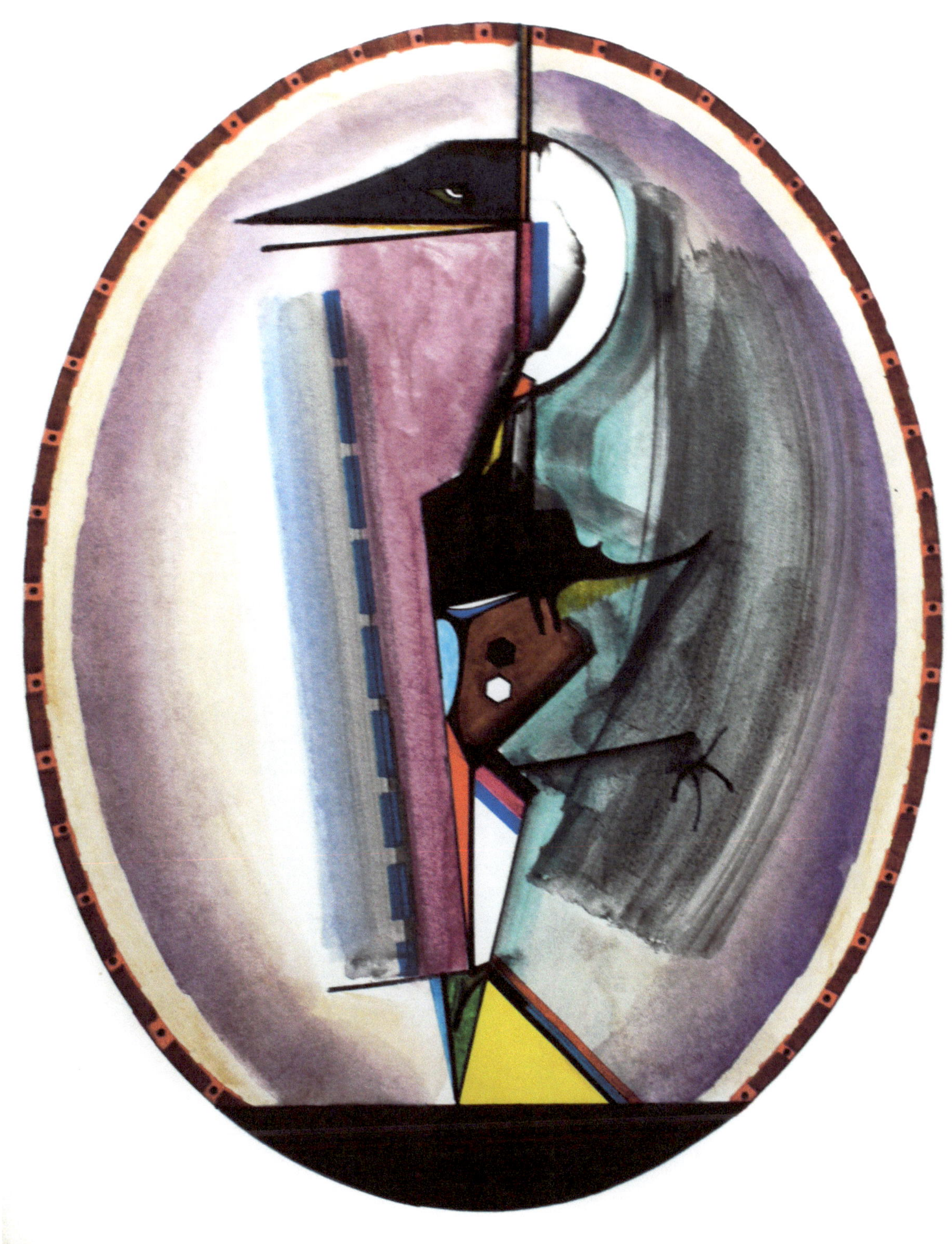

Untitled, 1973 mixed media oval drawing by Eugene Martin

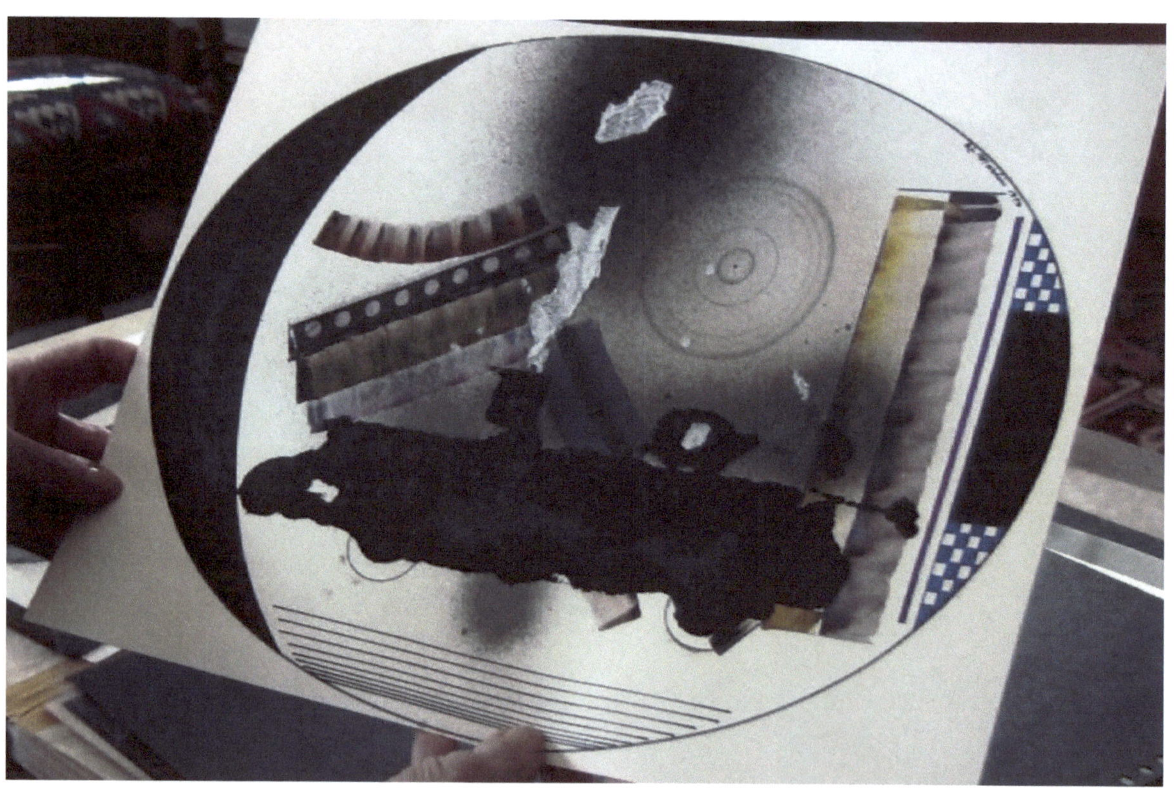

Untitled, 1972 mixed media oval drawing by Eugene Martin

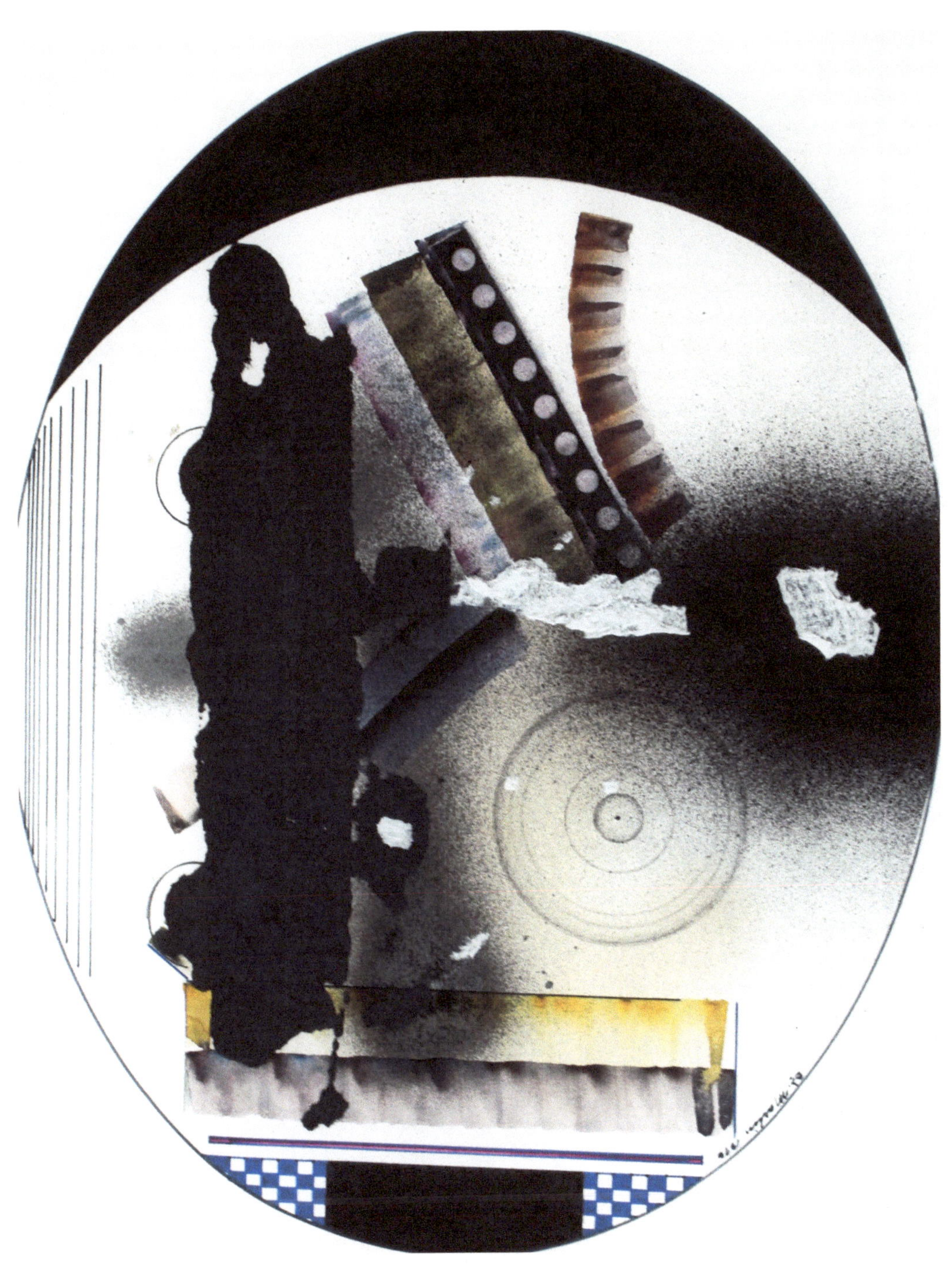

Untitled, 1972 mixed media oval drawing by Eugene Martin

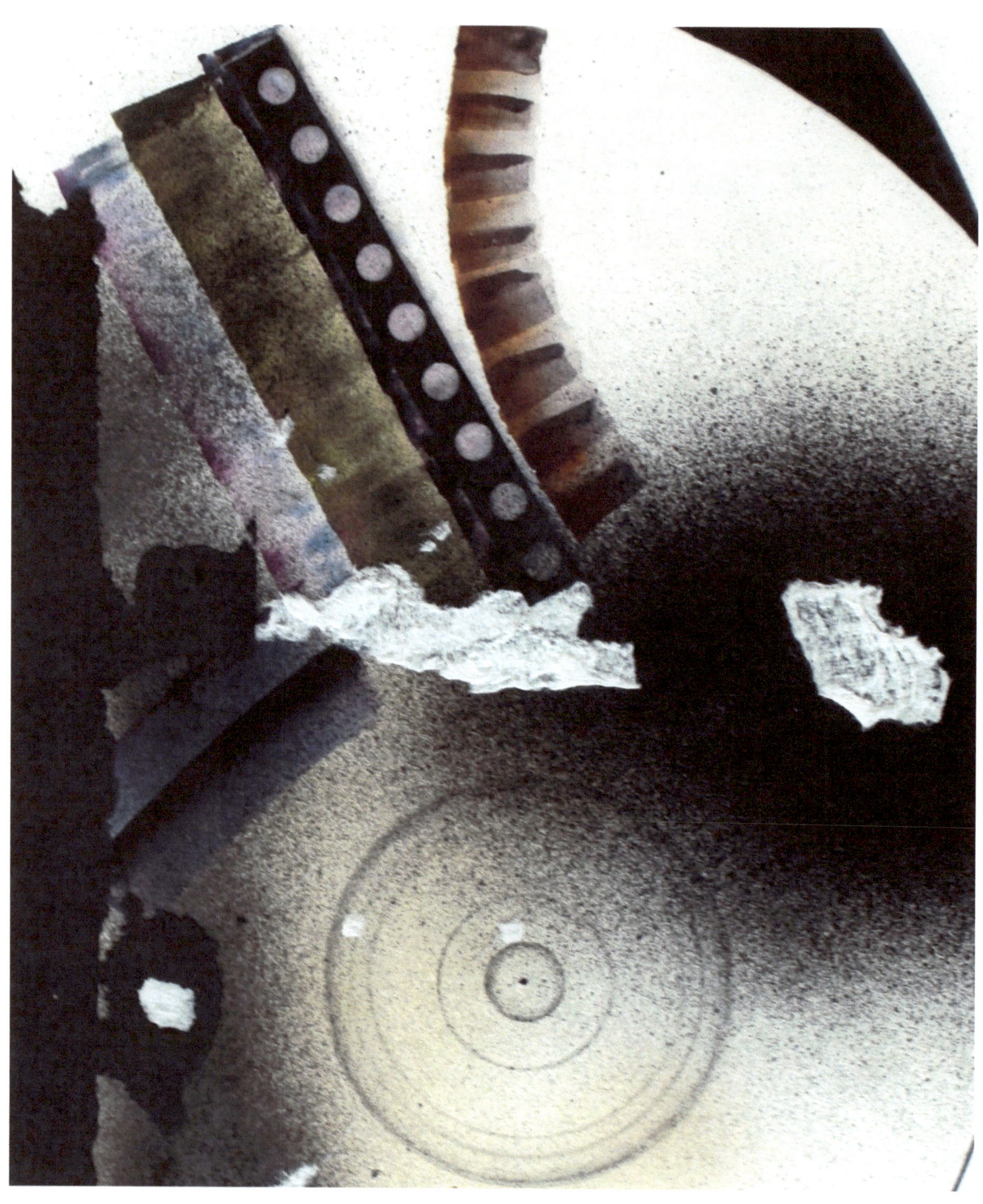

Detail of Untitled, 1972 mixed media oval drawing by Eugene Martin

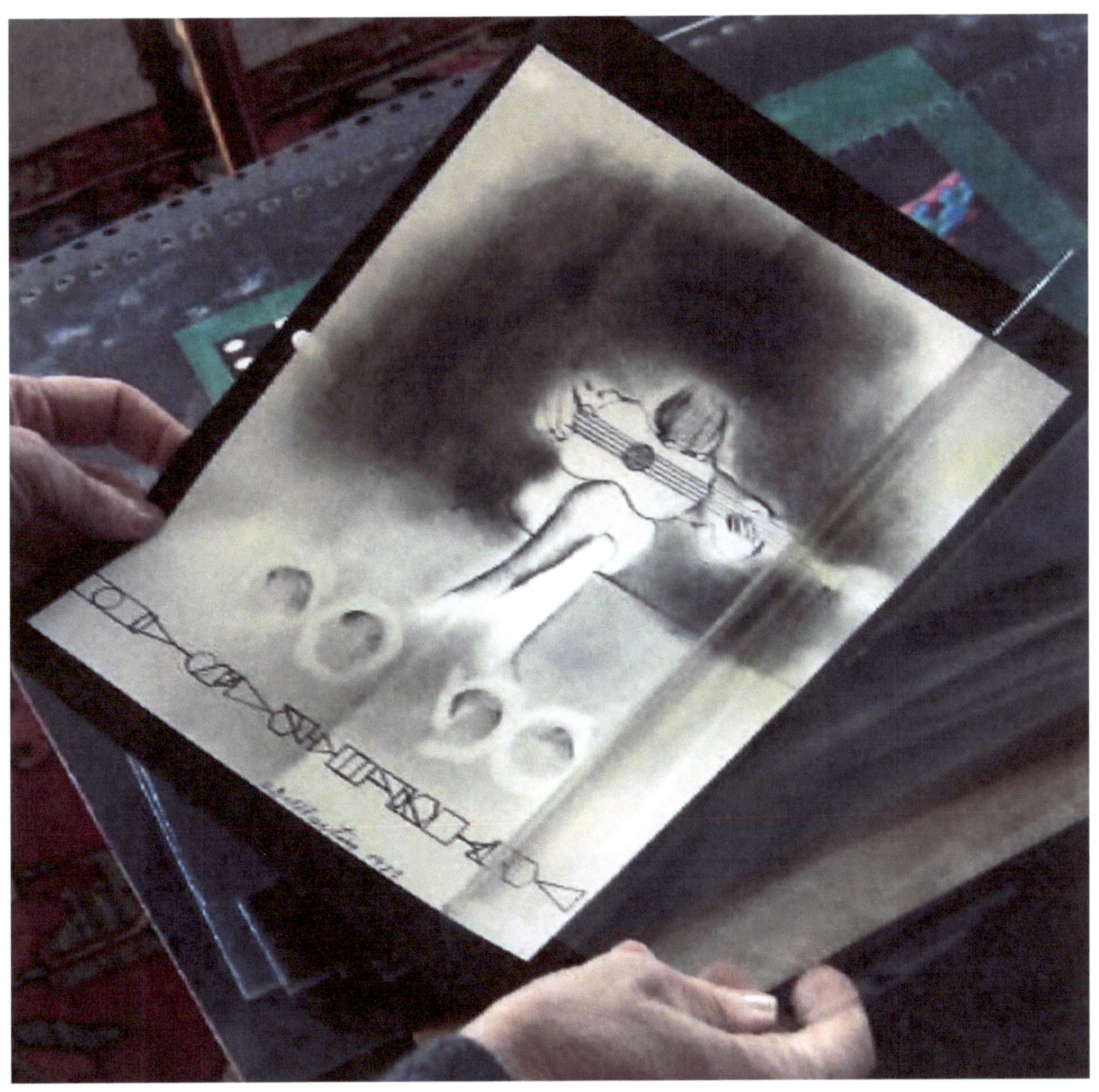

Untitled, 1977 graphite pencil drawing by Eugene Martin

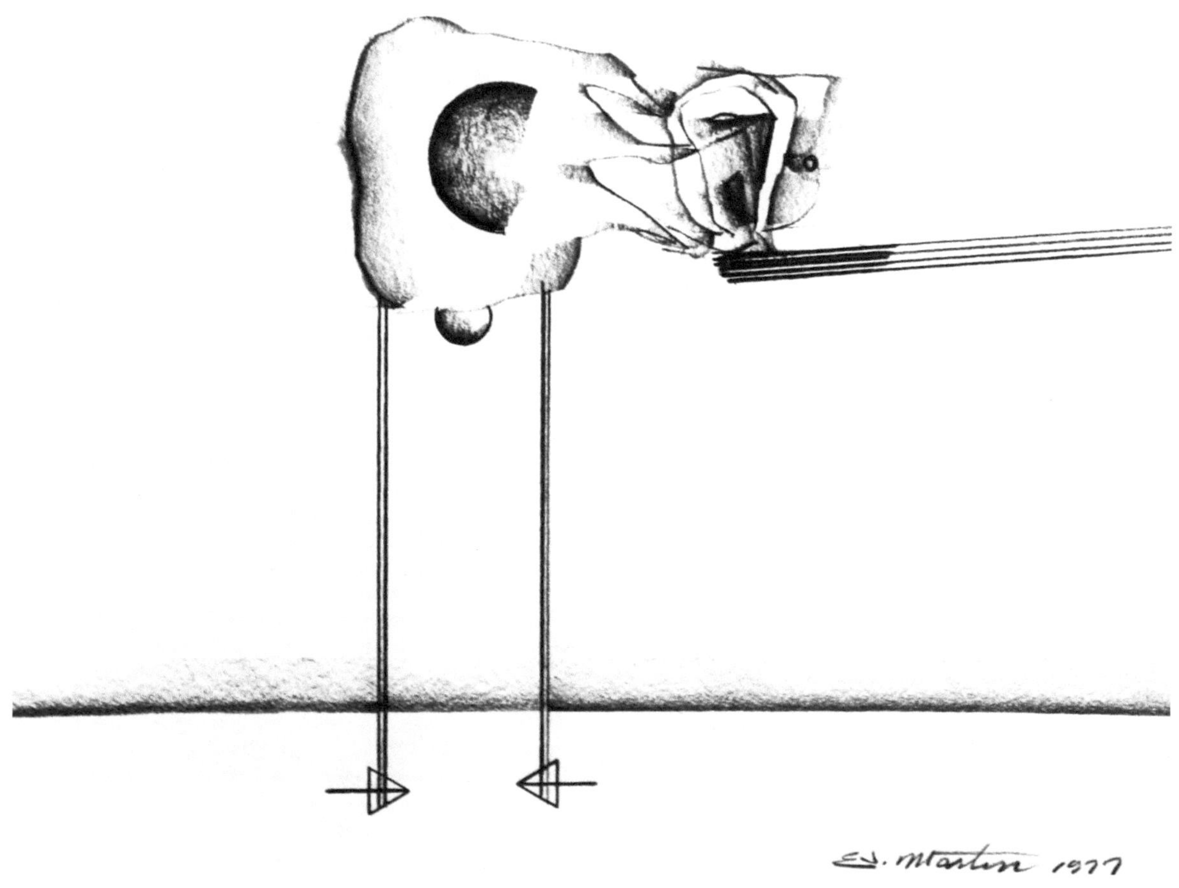

Untitled, 1977 graphite pencil drawing by Eugene Martin

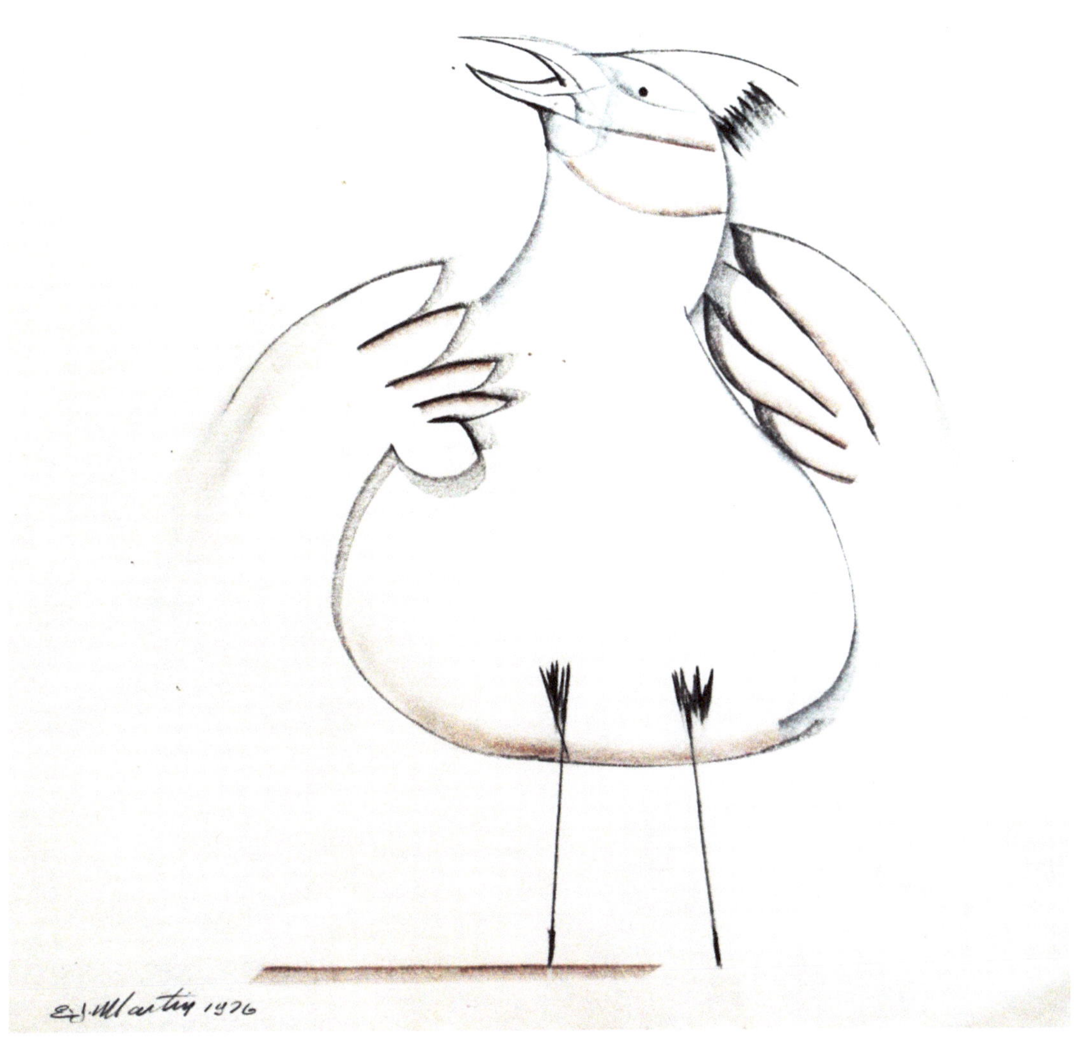

Untitled, 1976 color and graphite pencil drawing by Eugene Martin

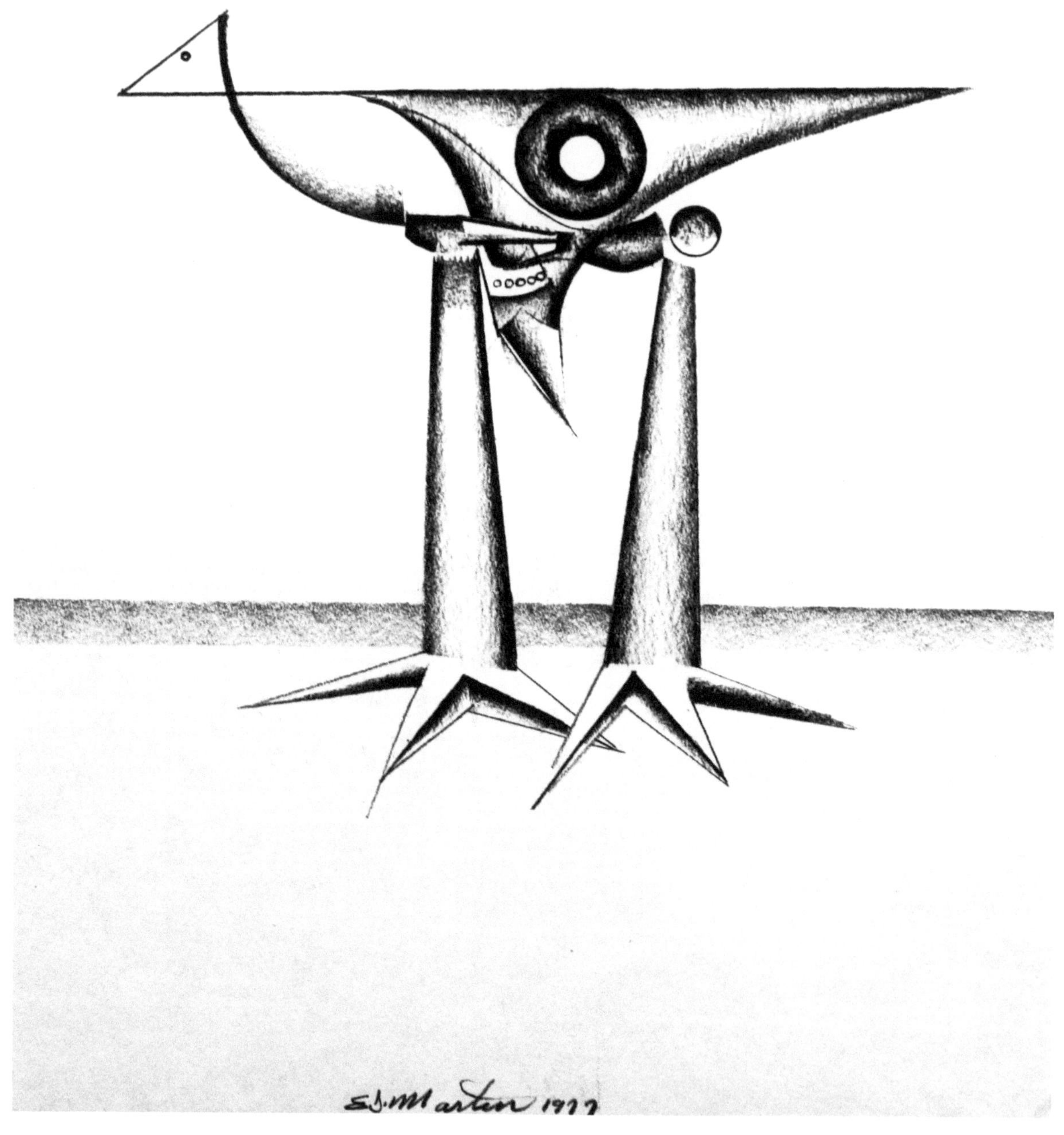

Untitled, 1977 graphite pencil drawing by Eugene Martin

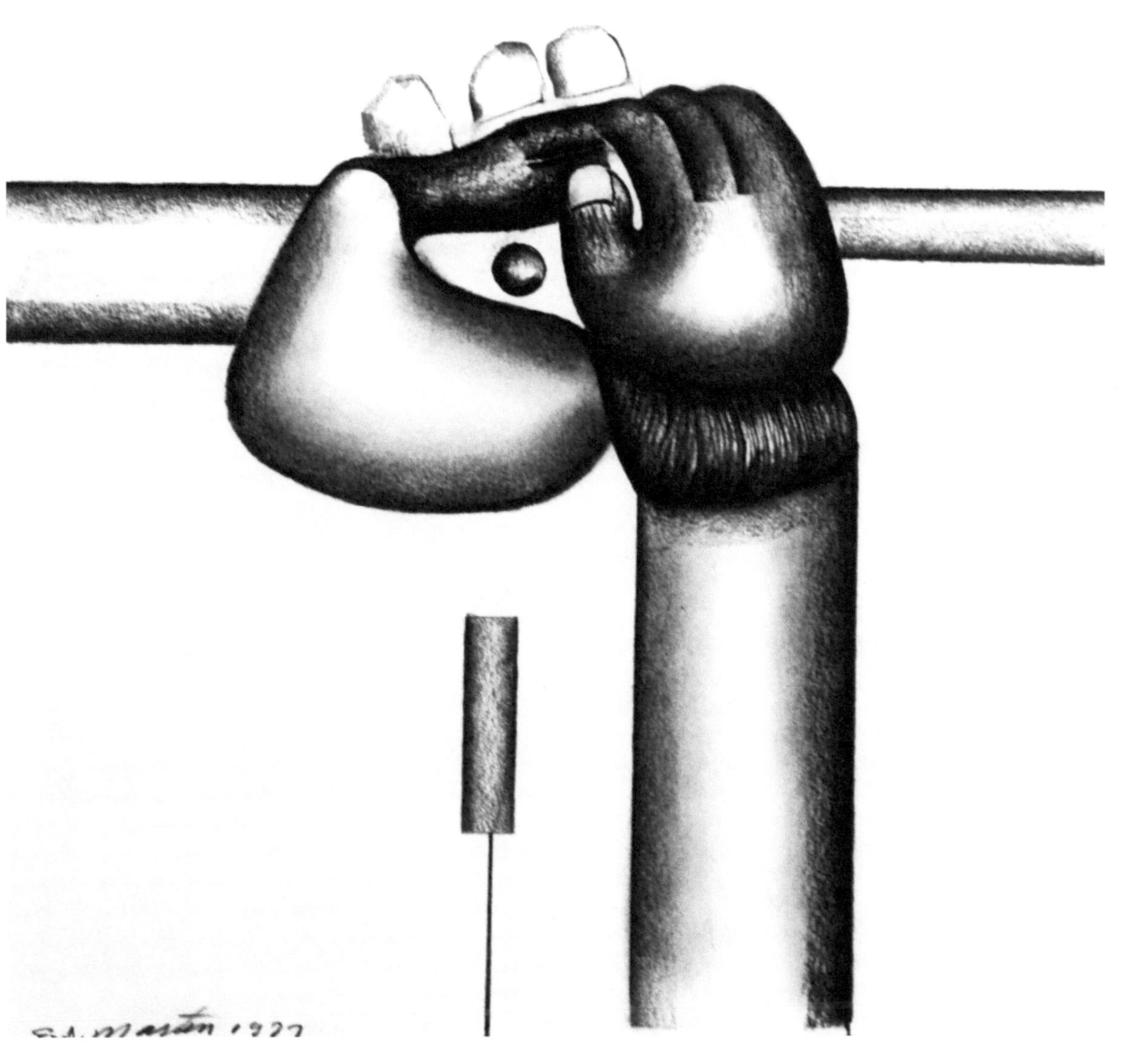

Untitled, 1977 graphite pencil drawing by Eugene Martin

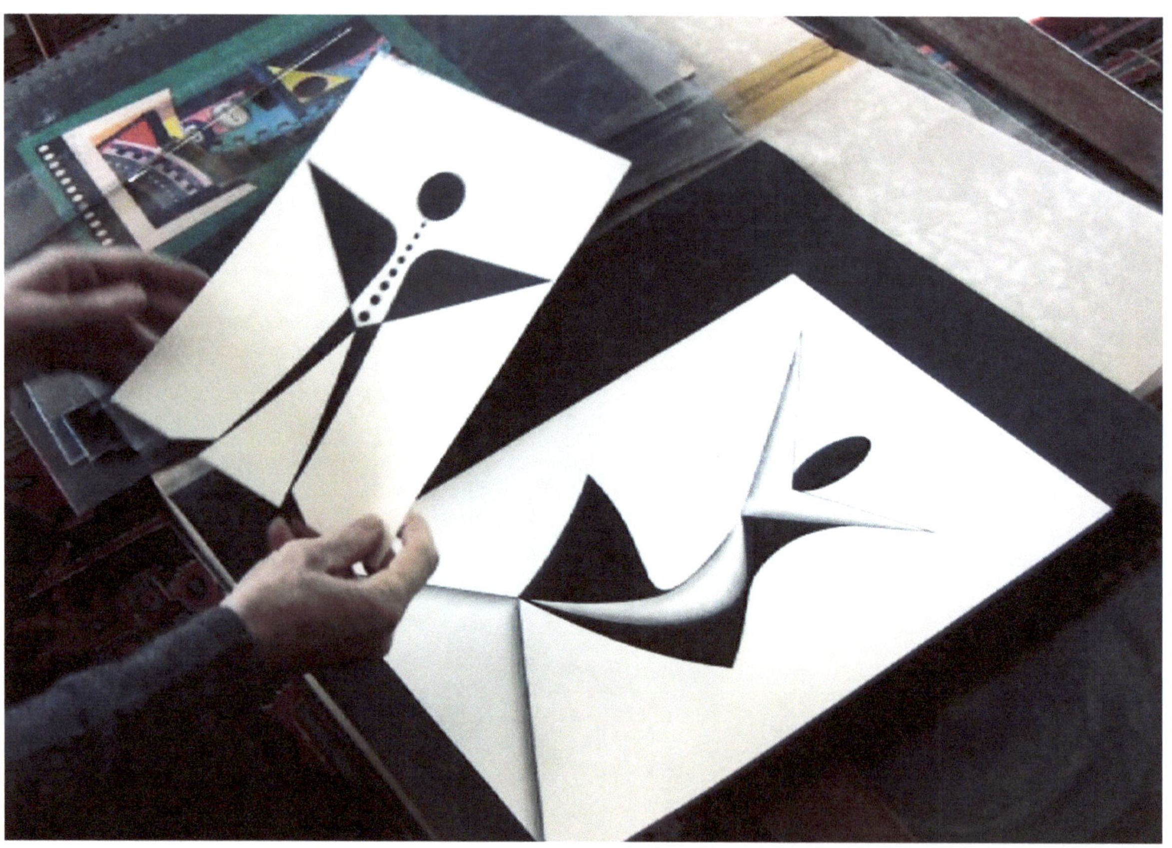

Untitled pen and ink drawings by Eugene Martin, at left from 1979, at right from 1986

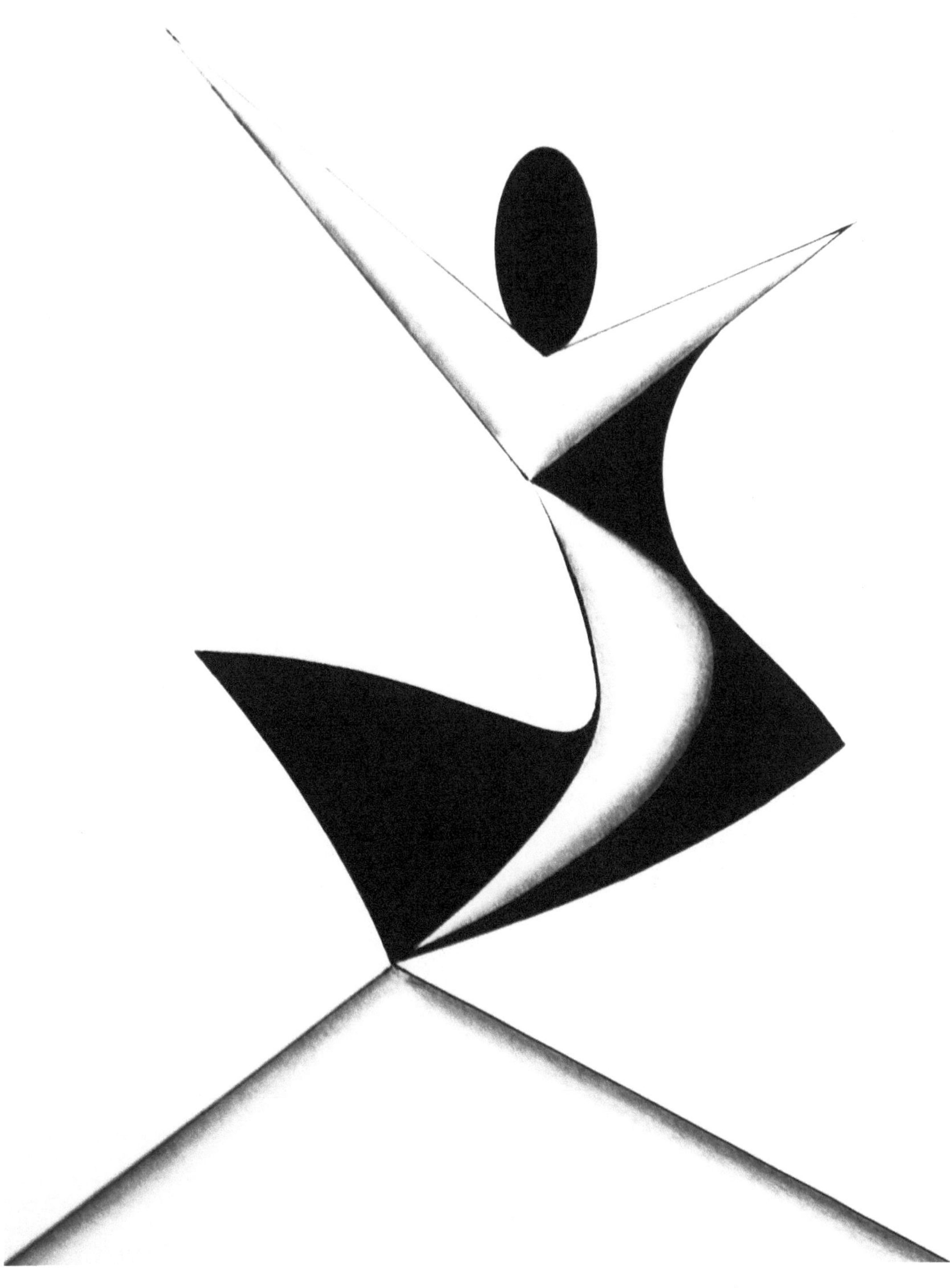

Untitled, 1986 pen and ink and graphite drawing on paper by Eugene Martin

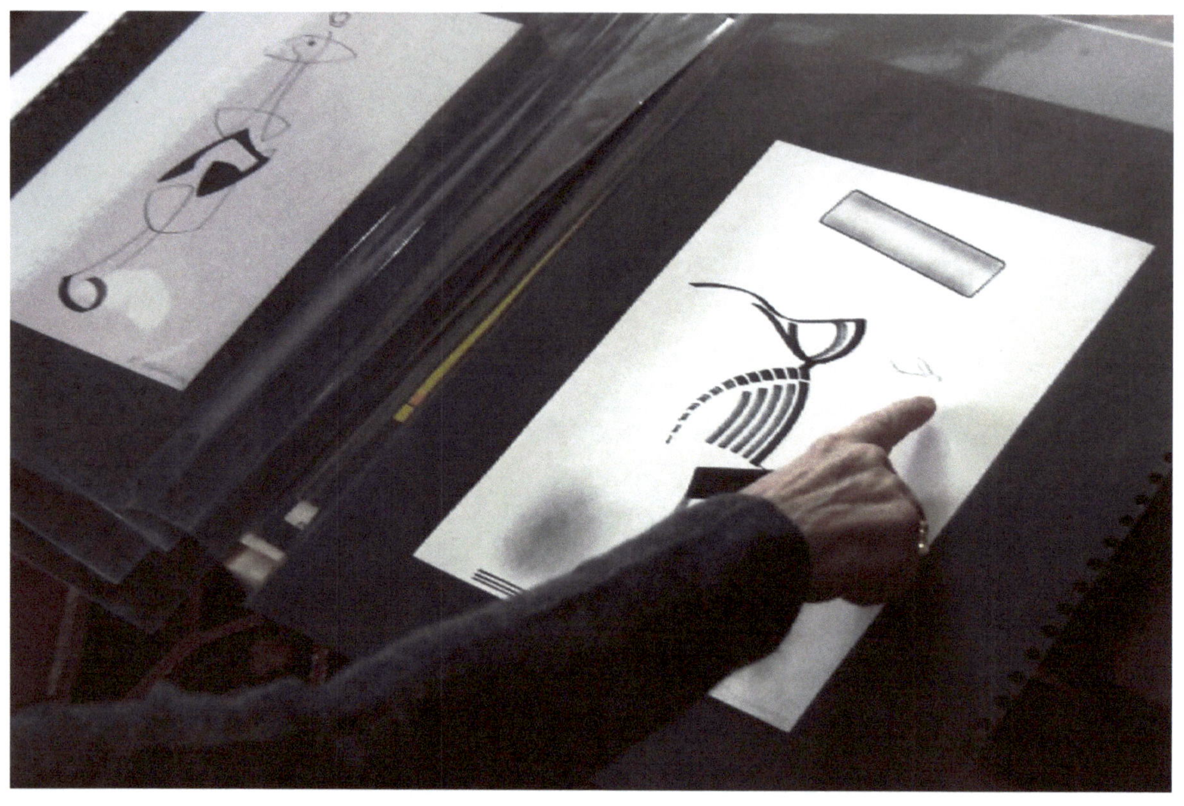

Isabel Taylor points to bird-like motif in an untitled 1976 felt-tip marker and pencil drawing by Eugene Martin

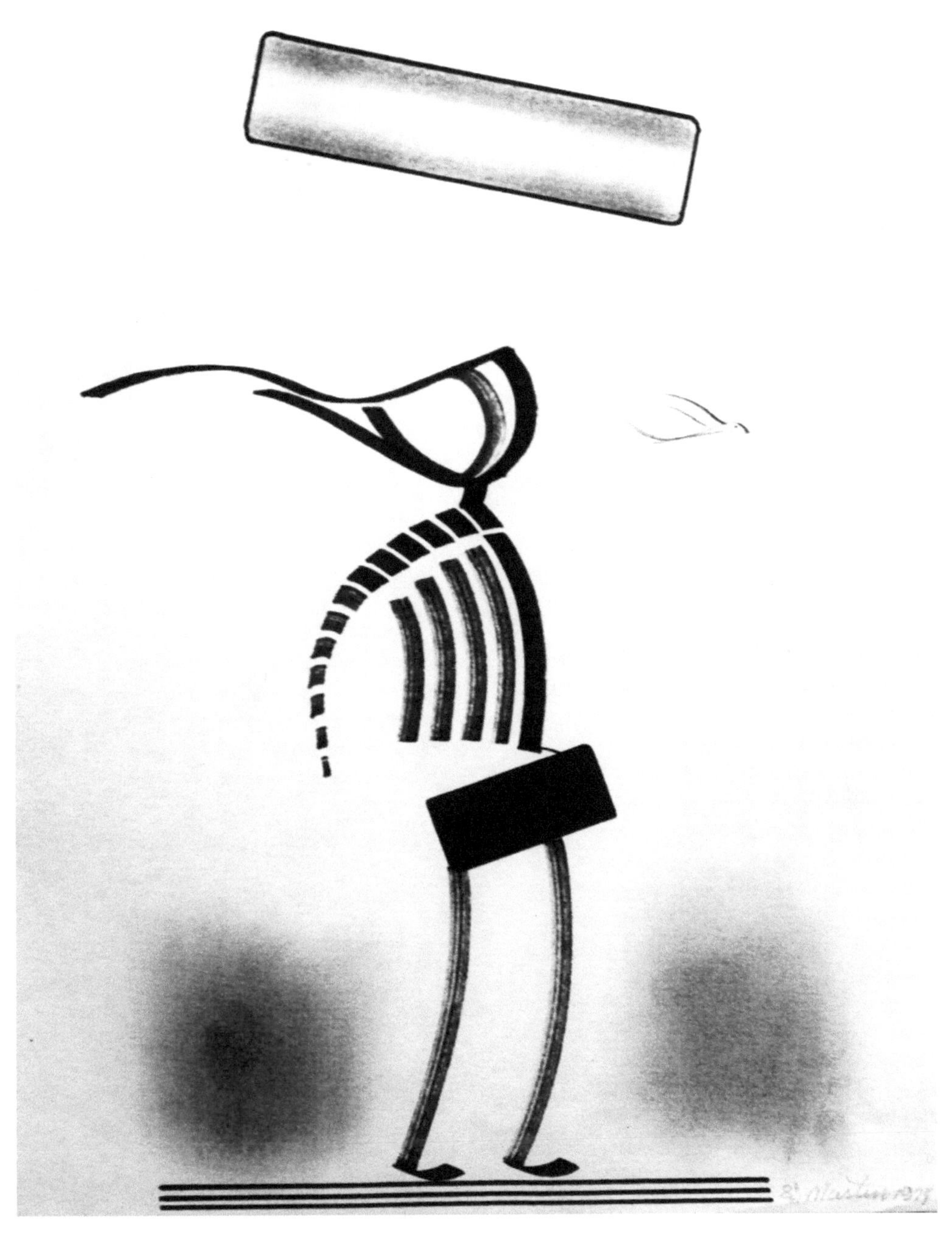

Untitled, 1974 felt-tip marker and graphite drawing by Eugene Martin

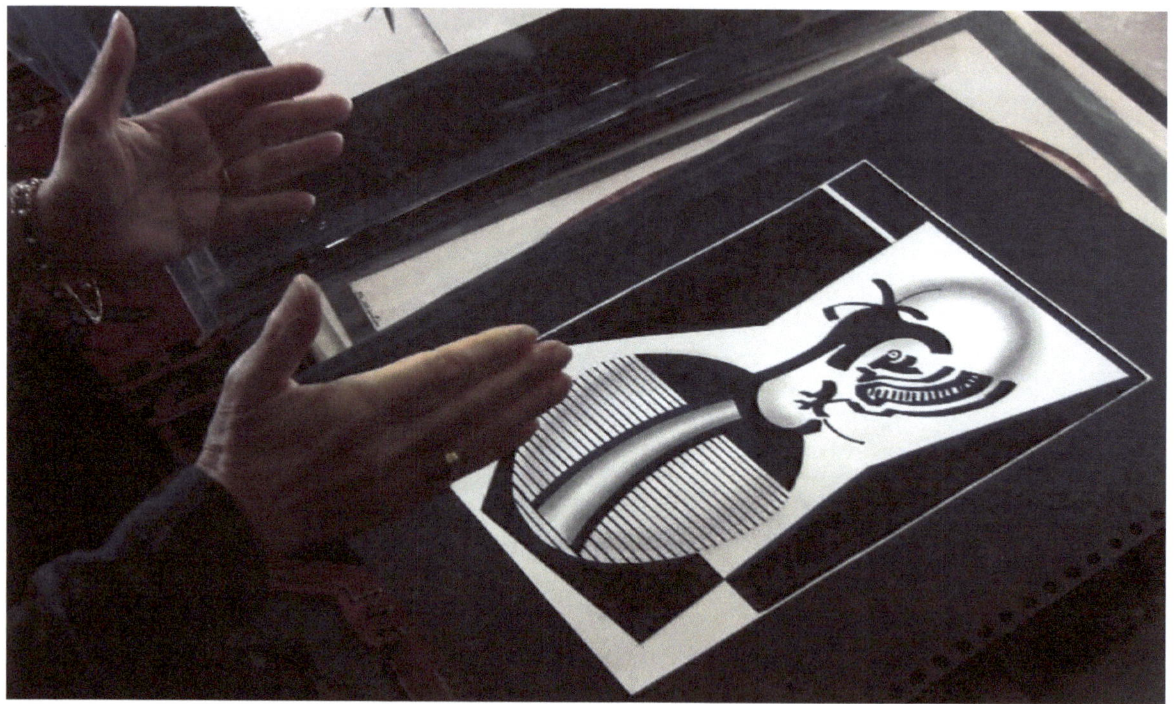

Isabel Taylor gestures in front of an untitled, 1974 felt-tip marker and graphite drawing by Eugene Martin

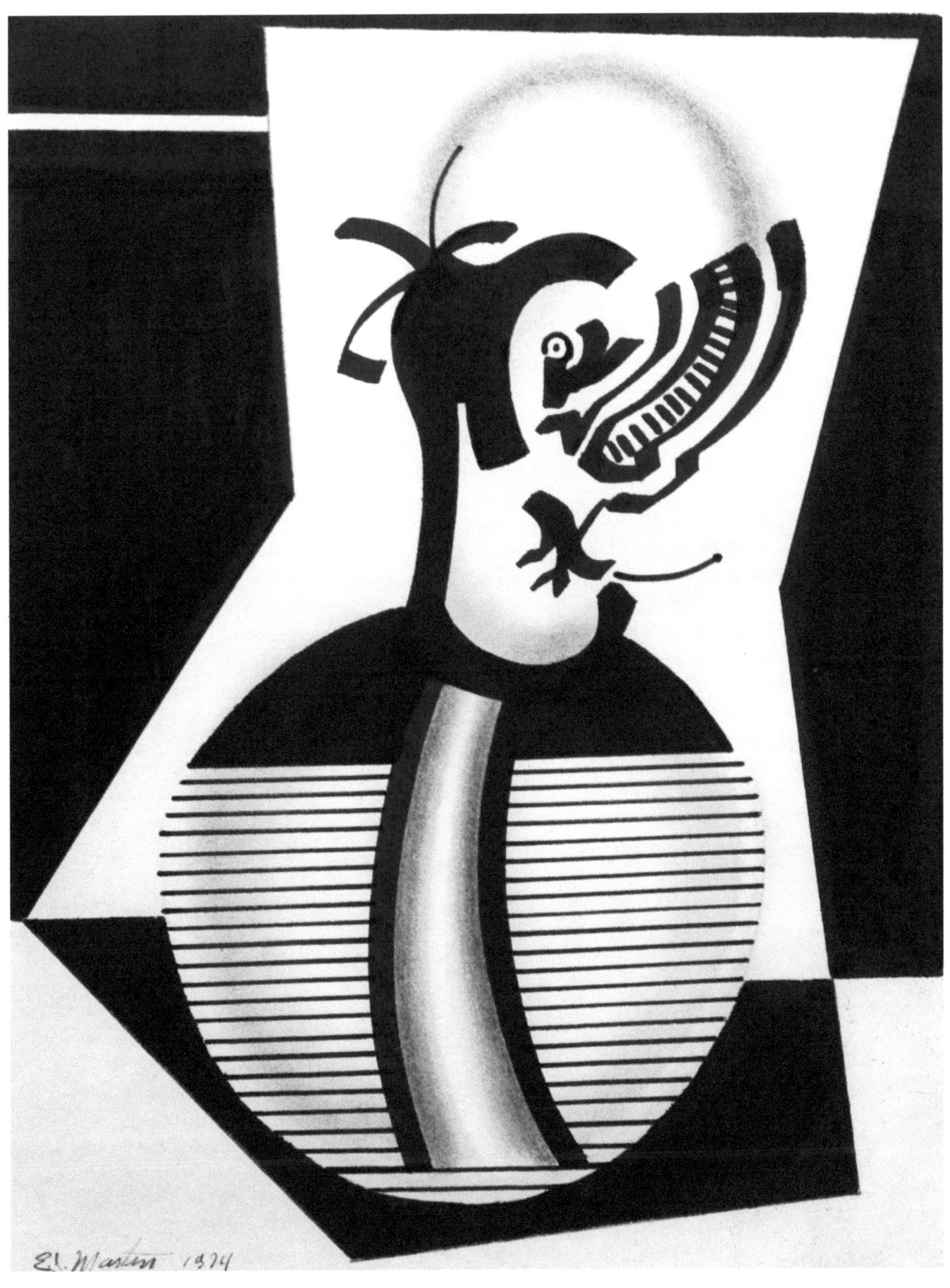

Untitled, 1974 felt-tip marker and graphite drawing by Eugene Martin

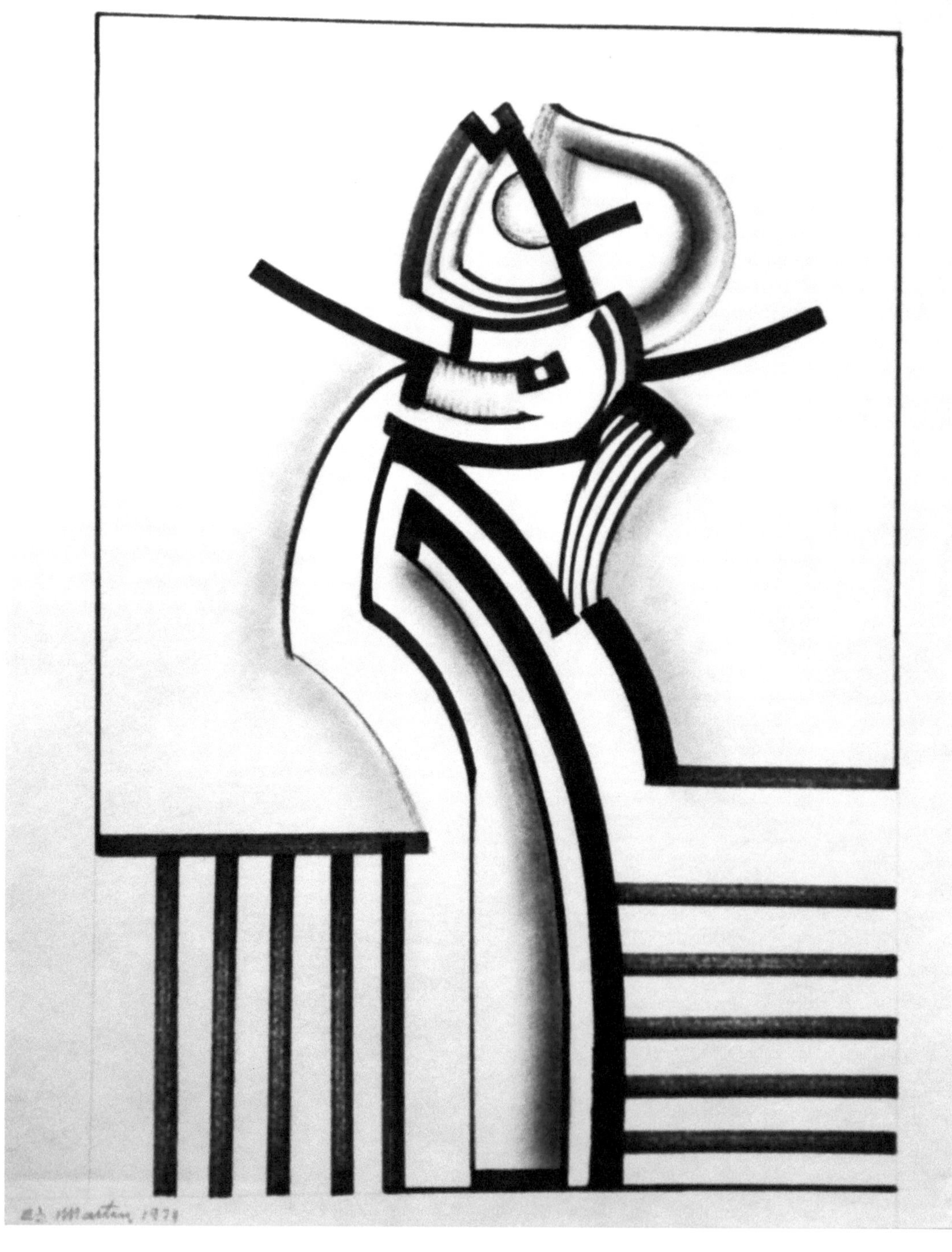

Untitled, 1974 felt-tip marker and graphite drawing by Eugene Martin

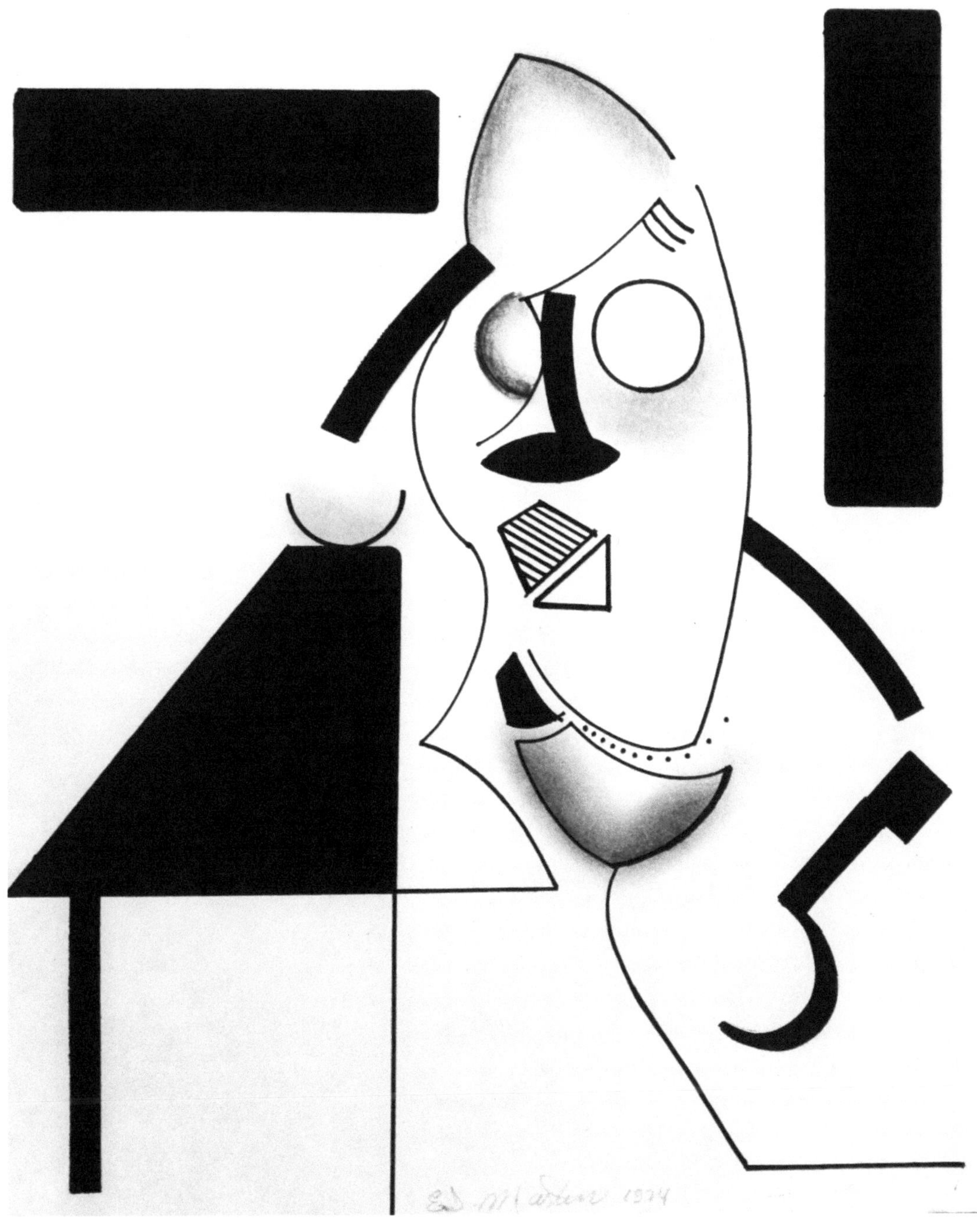

Untitled, 1974 felt-tip marker and graphite drawing by Eugene Martin

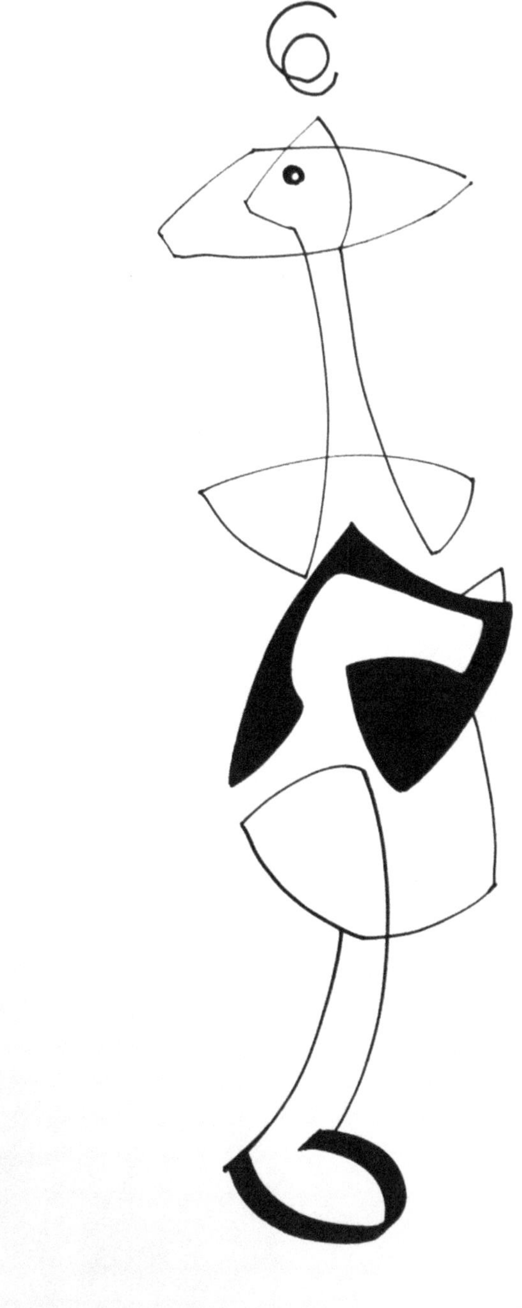

Untitled, 1974 pen and ink drawing by Eugene Martin

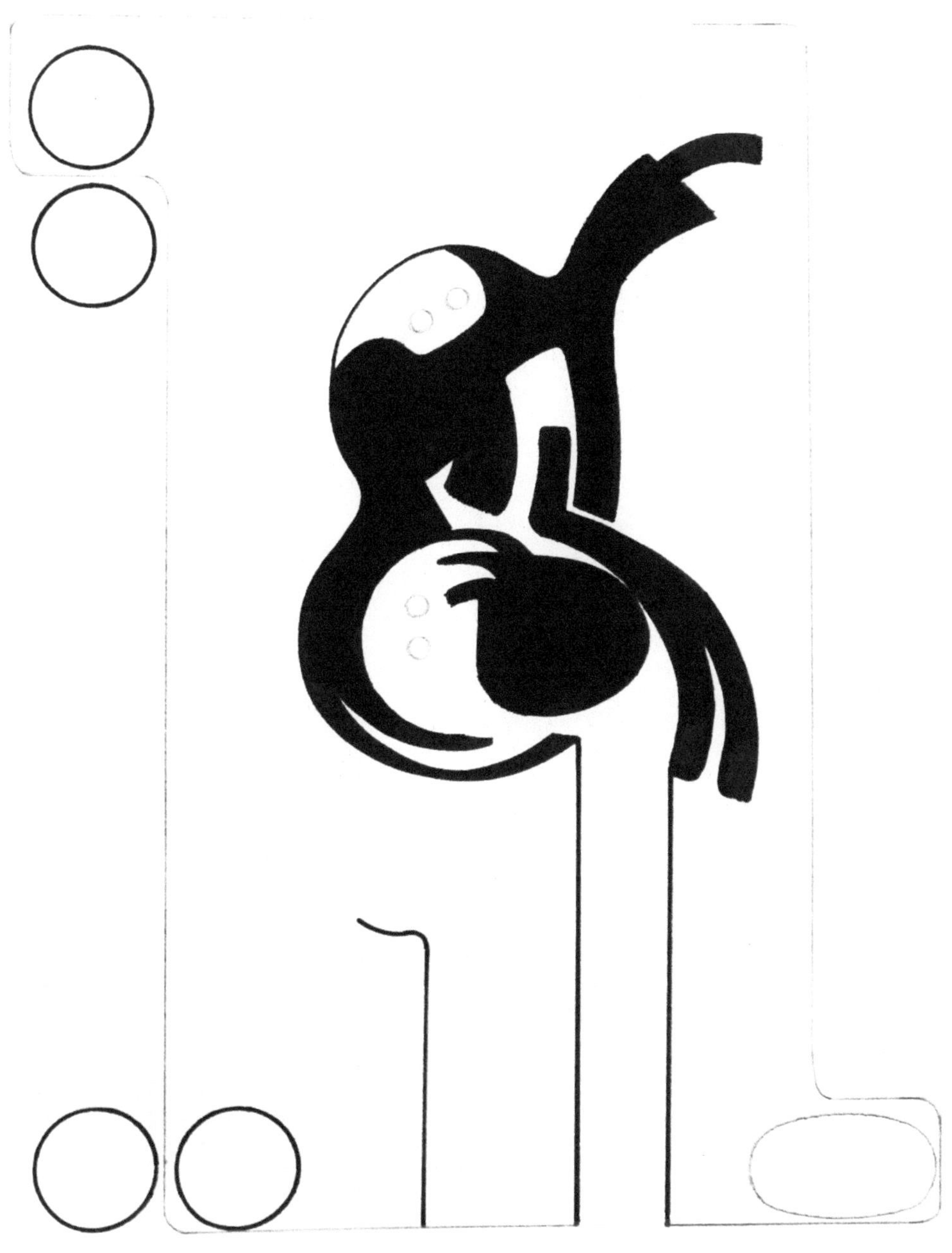

Untitled, 1974 pen and ink drawing by Eugene Martin

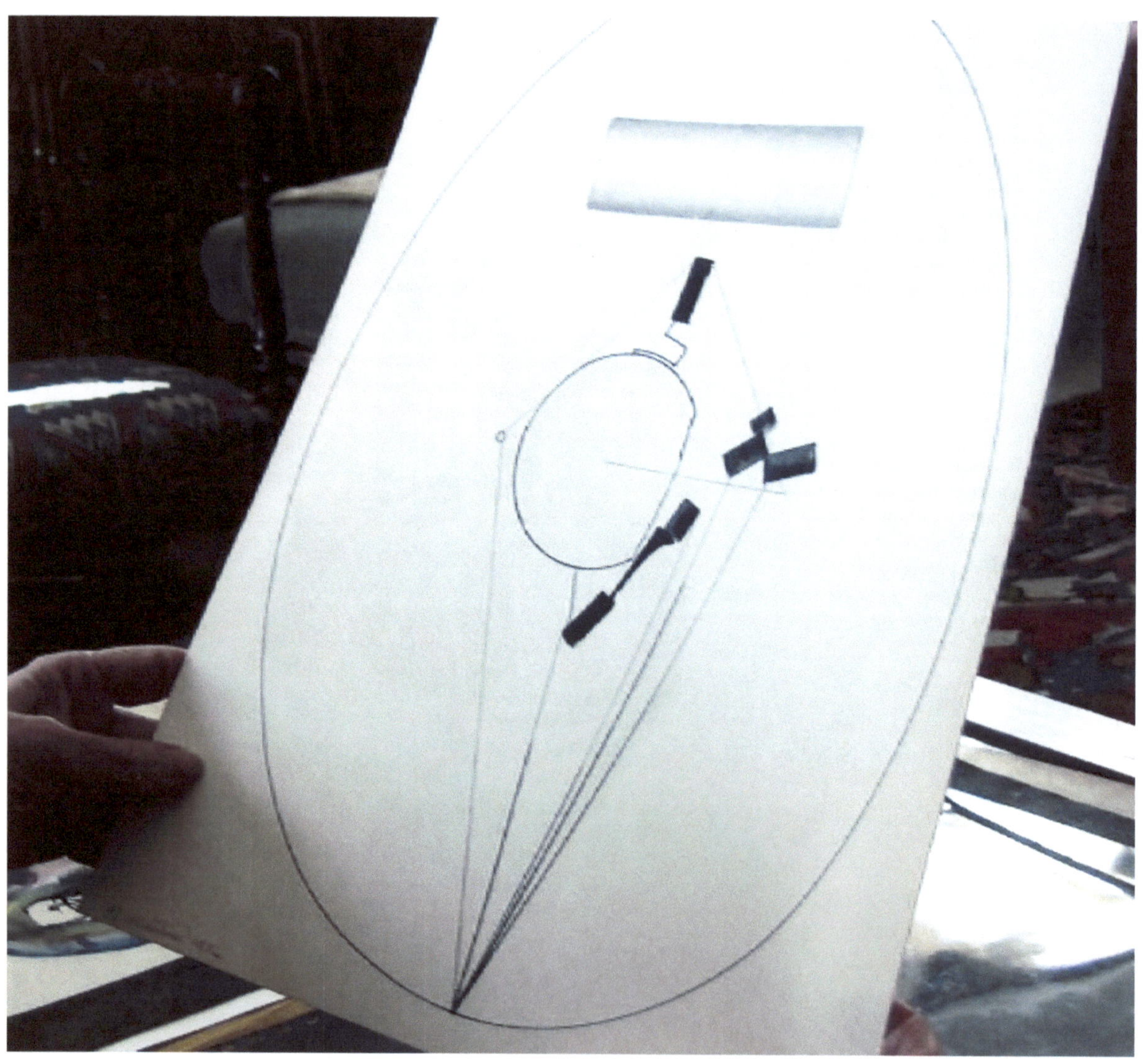

Untitled, 1971 oval pen and ink and graphite pencil drawing by Eugene Martin

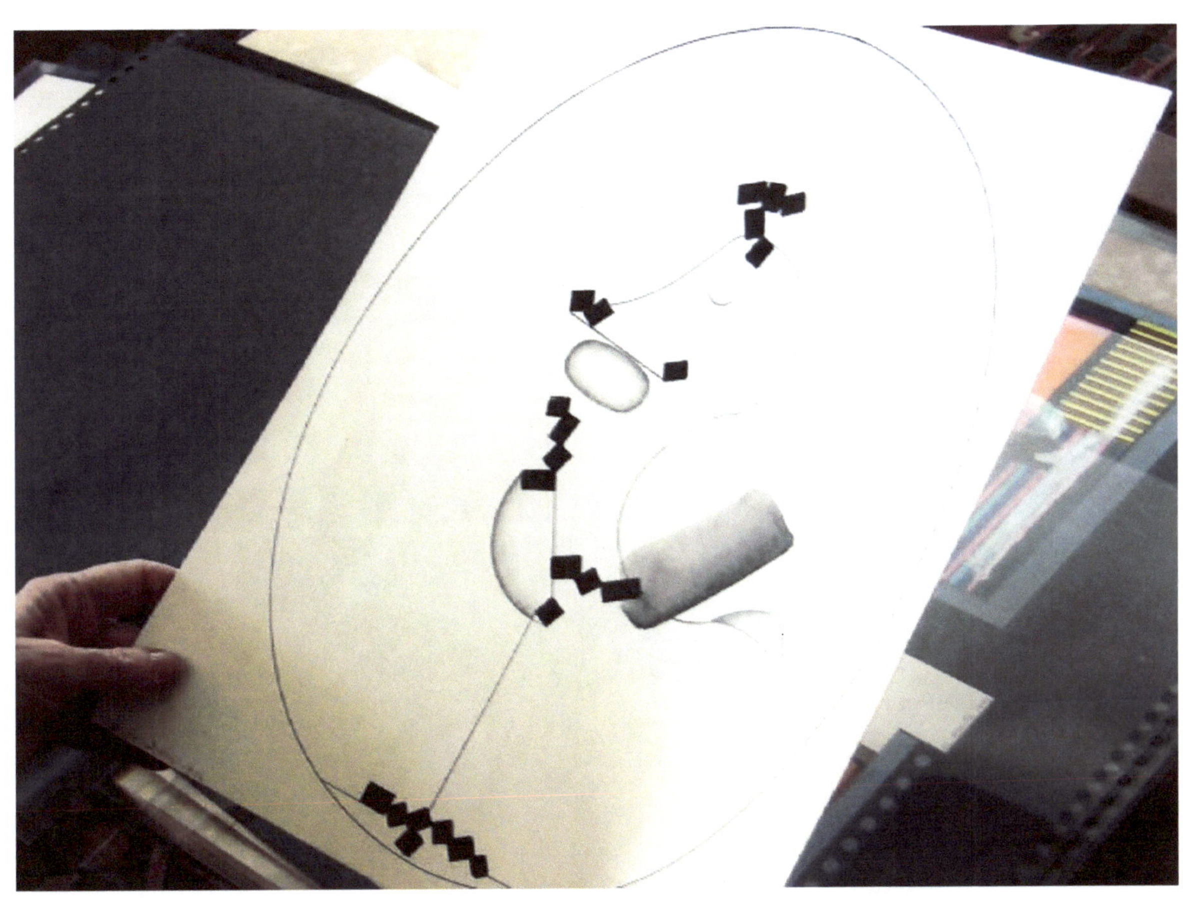

Untitled, 1971 oval pen and ink and graphite pencil drawing by Eugene Martin

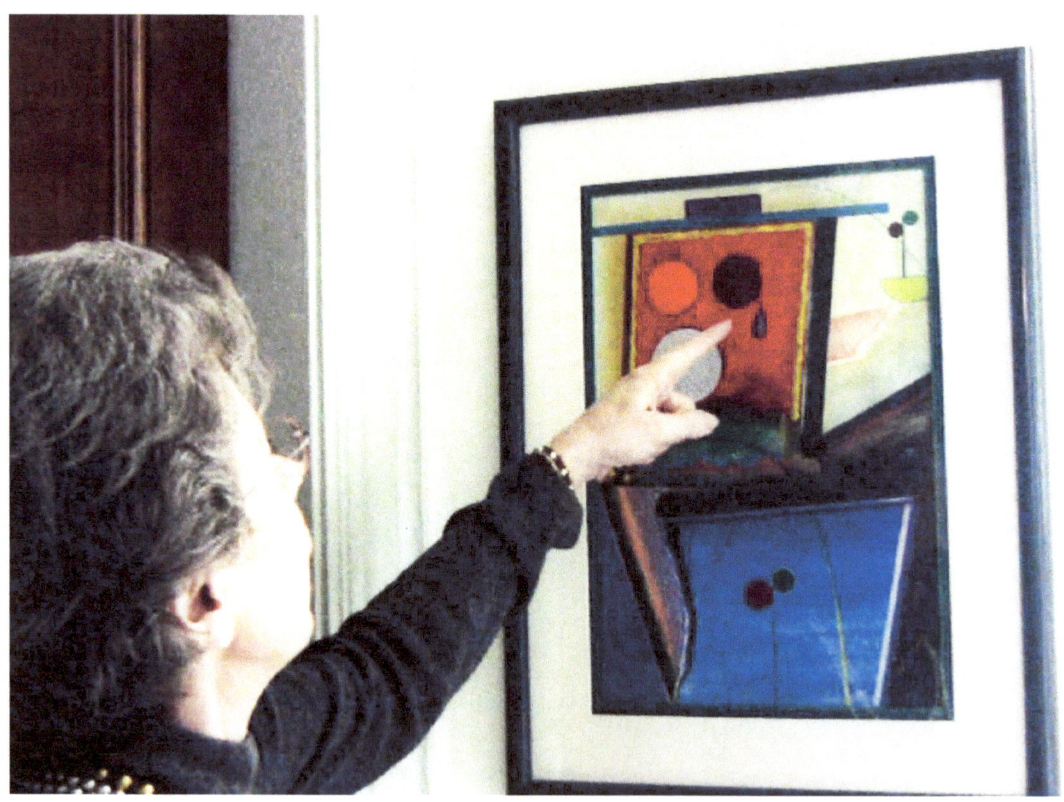

Isabel Taylor points to a tear in Eugene Martin's untitled 1989 mixed media work on paper in her kitchen in Washington D.C.

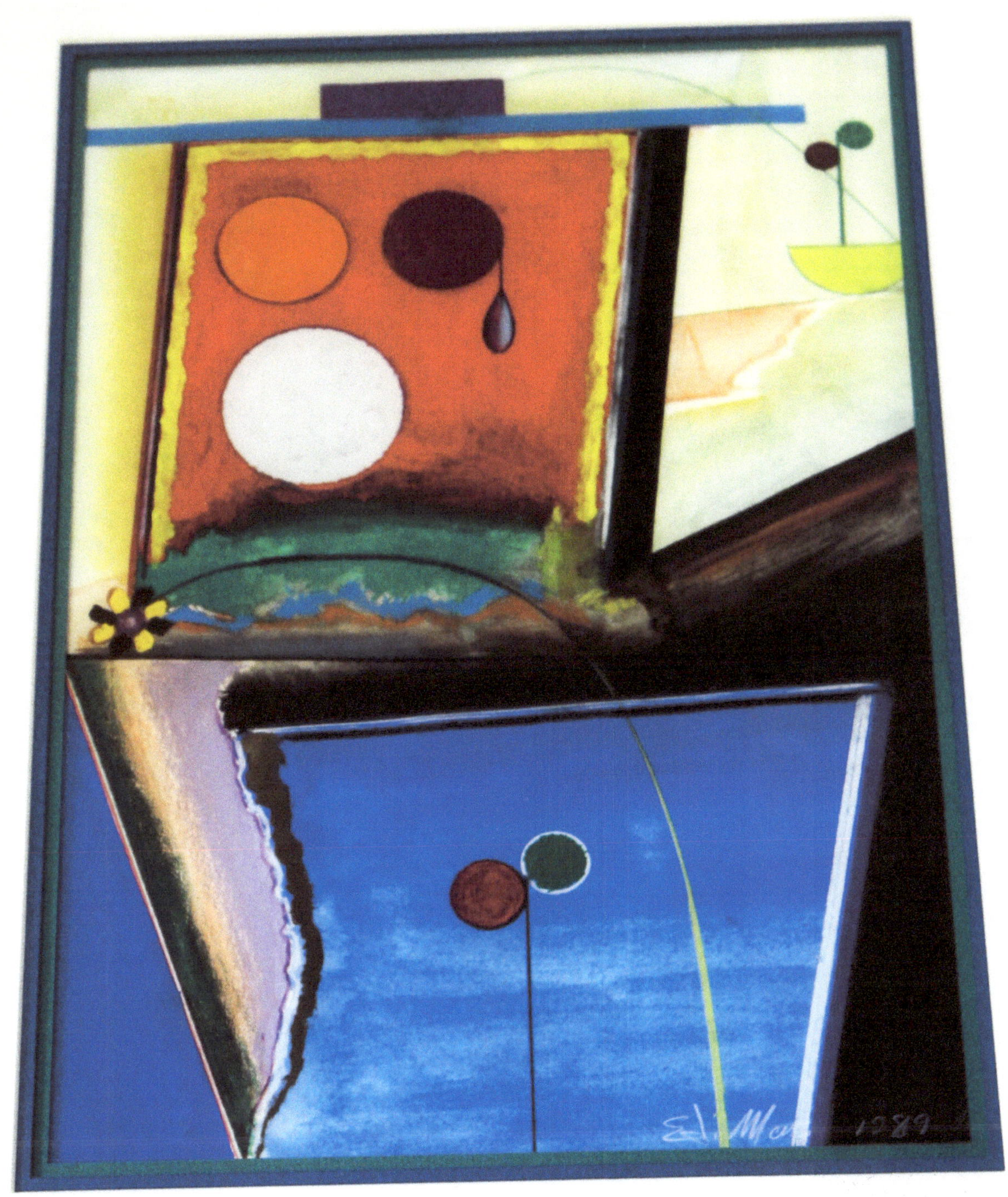

Untitled, 1989 mixed media work on paper by Eugene Martin

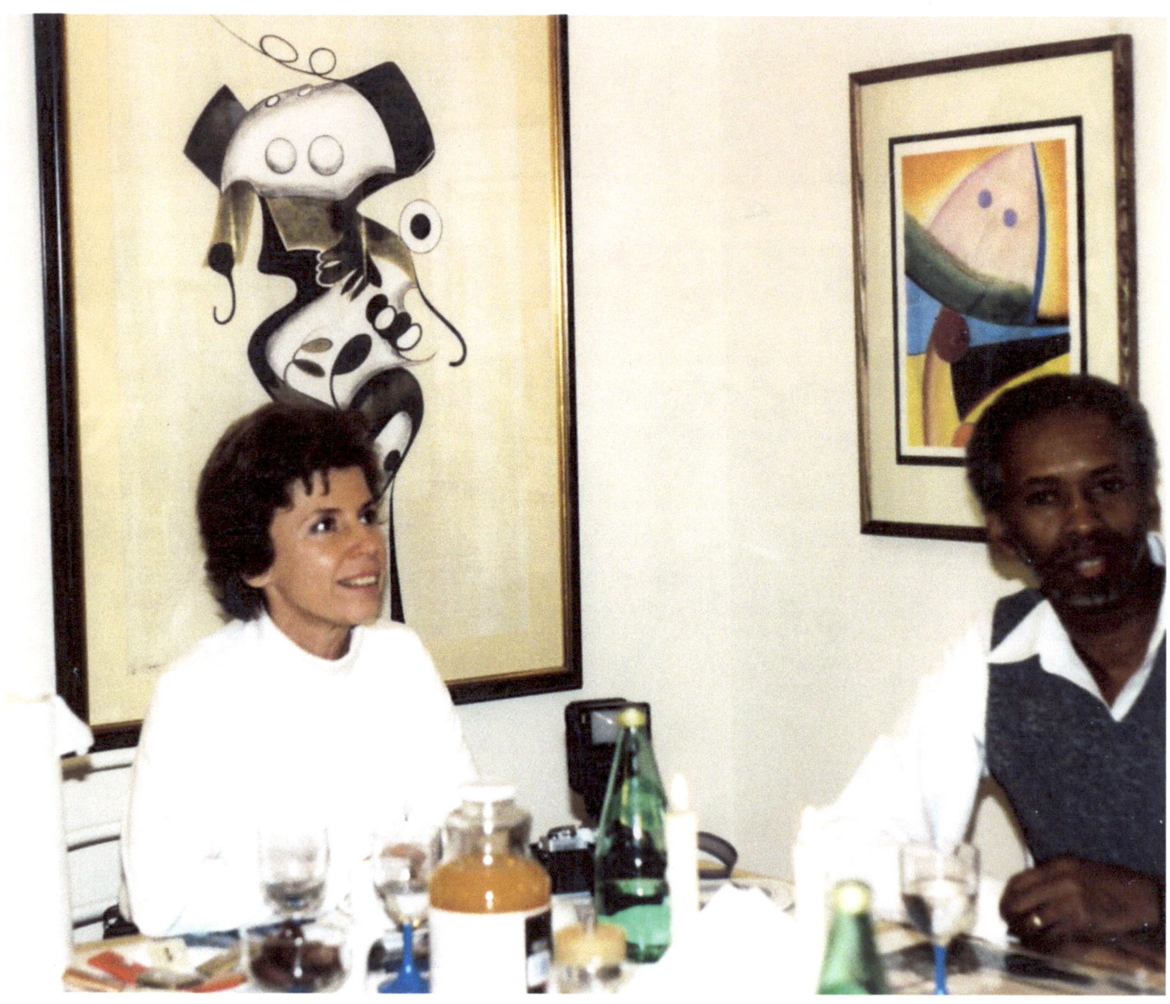

Isabel Taylor and Eugene Martin in Eugene and Suzanne's apartment in Washington D.C., 1989

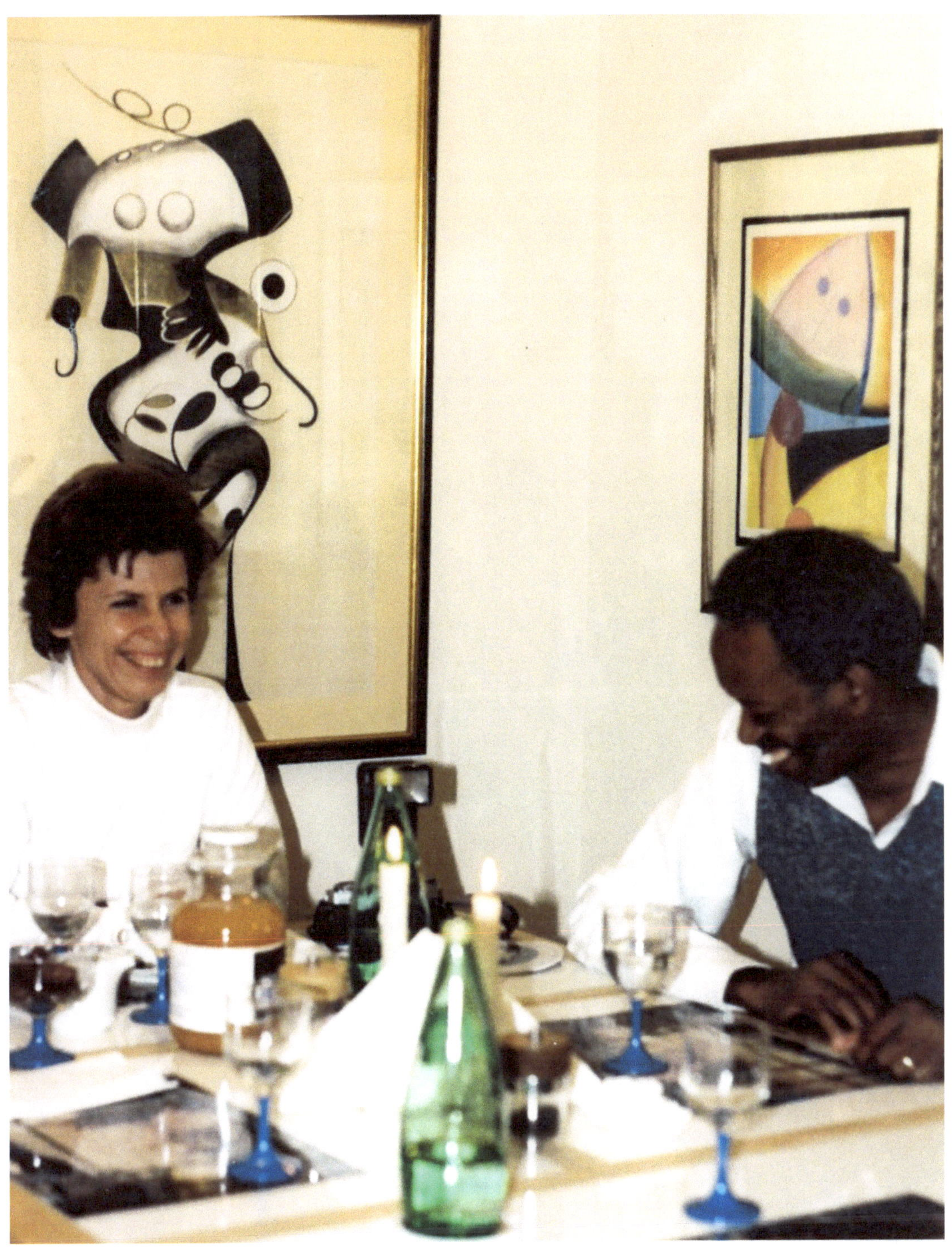

Isabel Taylor and Eugene Martin sharing a laugh, Washington D.C., 1989

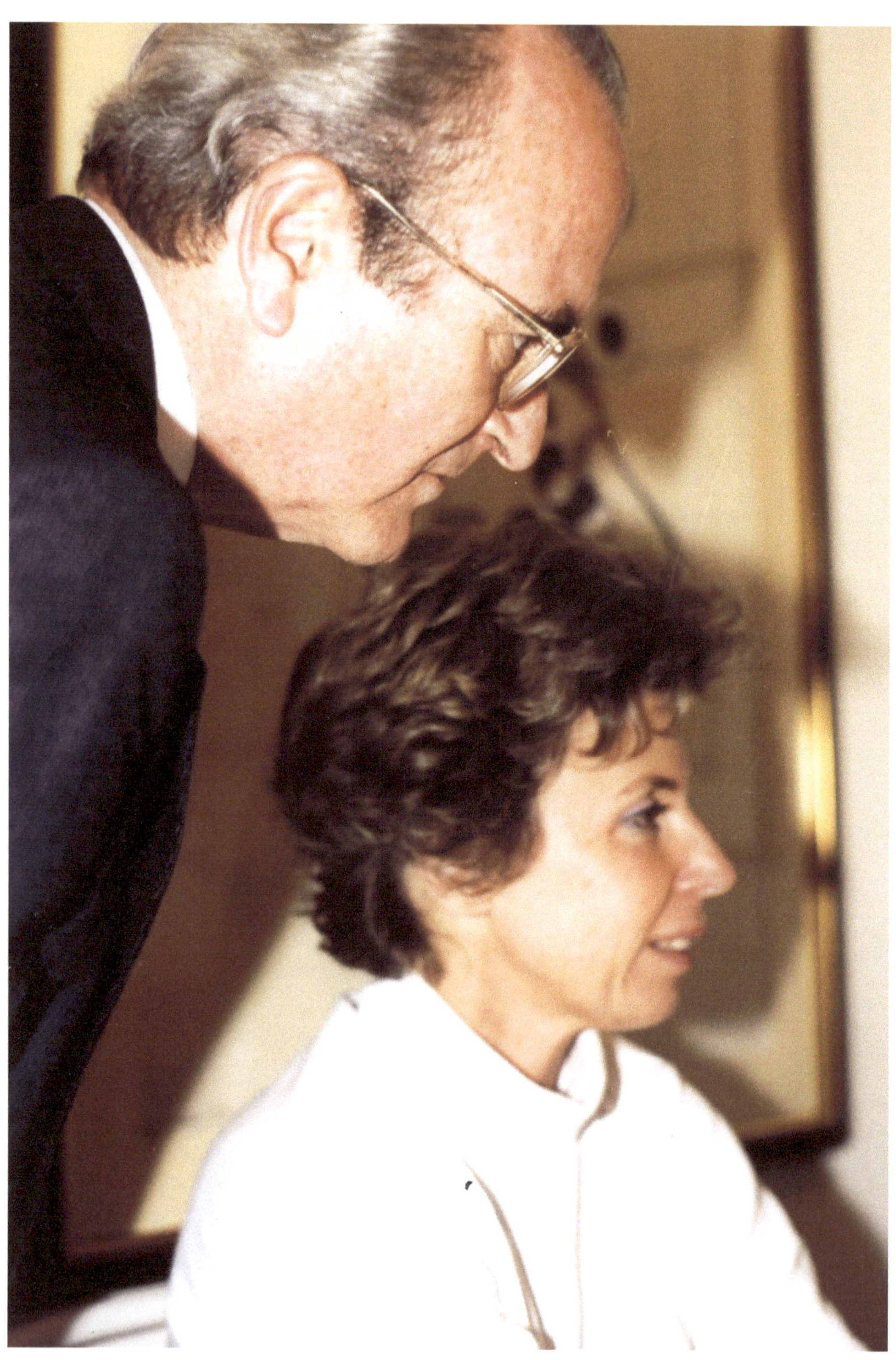

Isabel and David Taylor looking at an artwork of Eugene Martin, Washington D.C., 1989

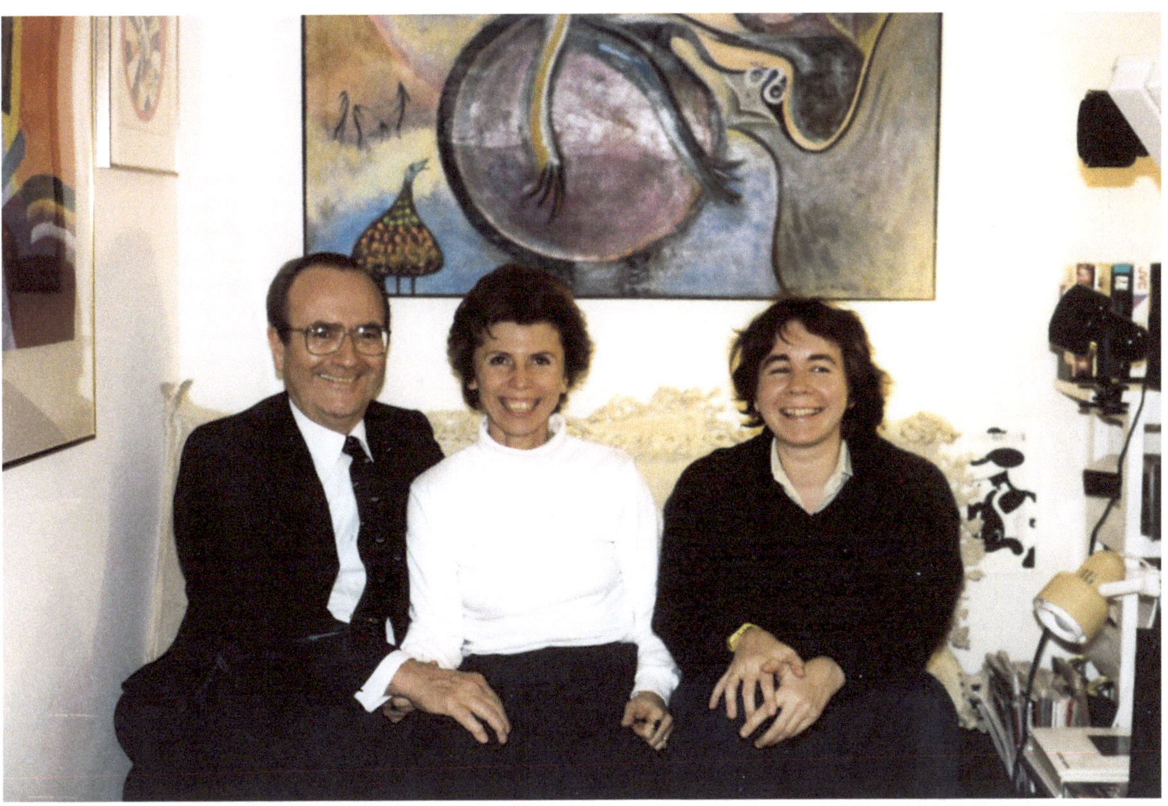

David Taylor, Isabel Taylor and Suzanne Fredericq sitting below a painting by Eugene Martin, Washington D.C., 1989

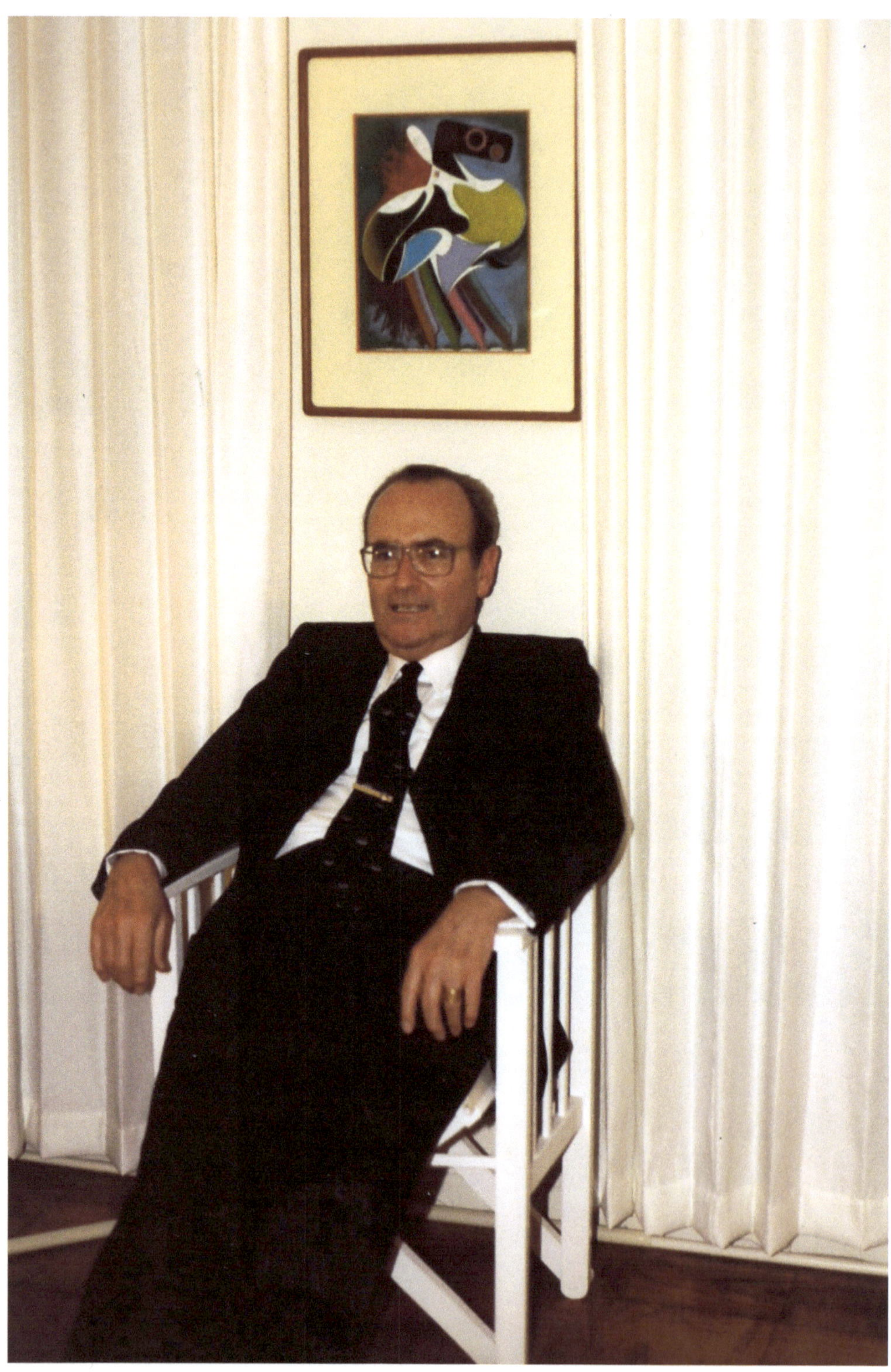

David Taylor sitting below a painting by Eugene Martin in Eugene's apartment in Washington D.C., 1989

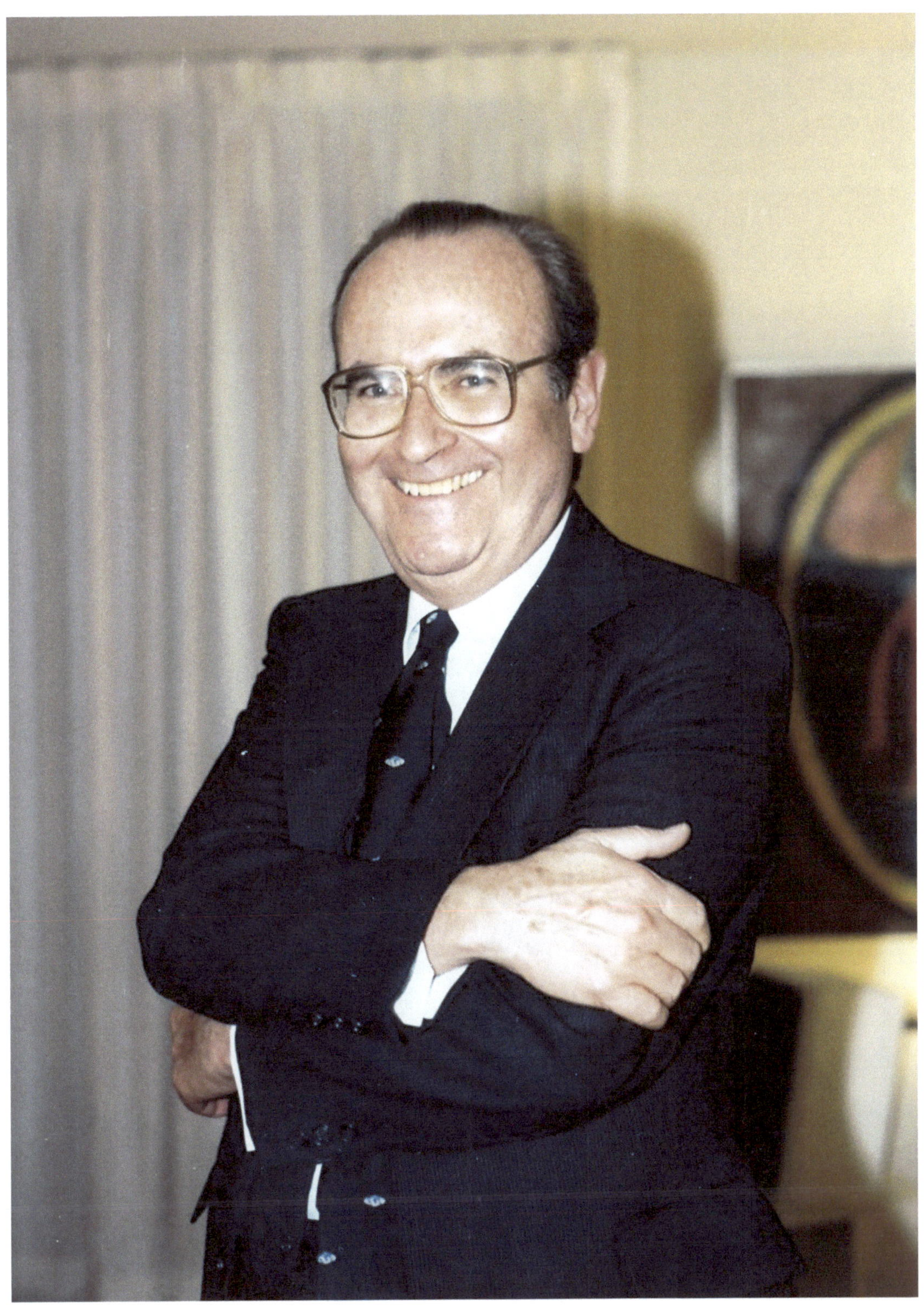

David Taylor in Eugene and Suzanne's apartment, Washington D.C., 1989

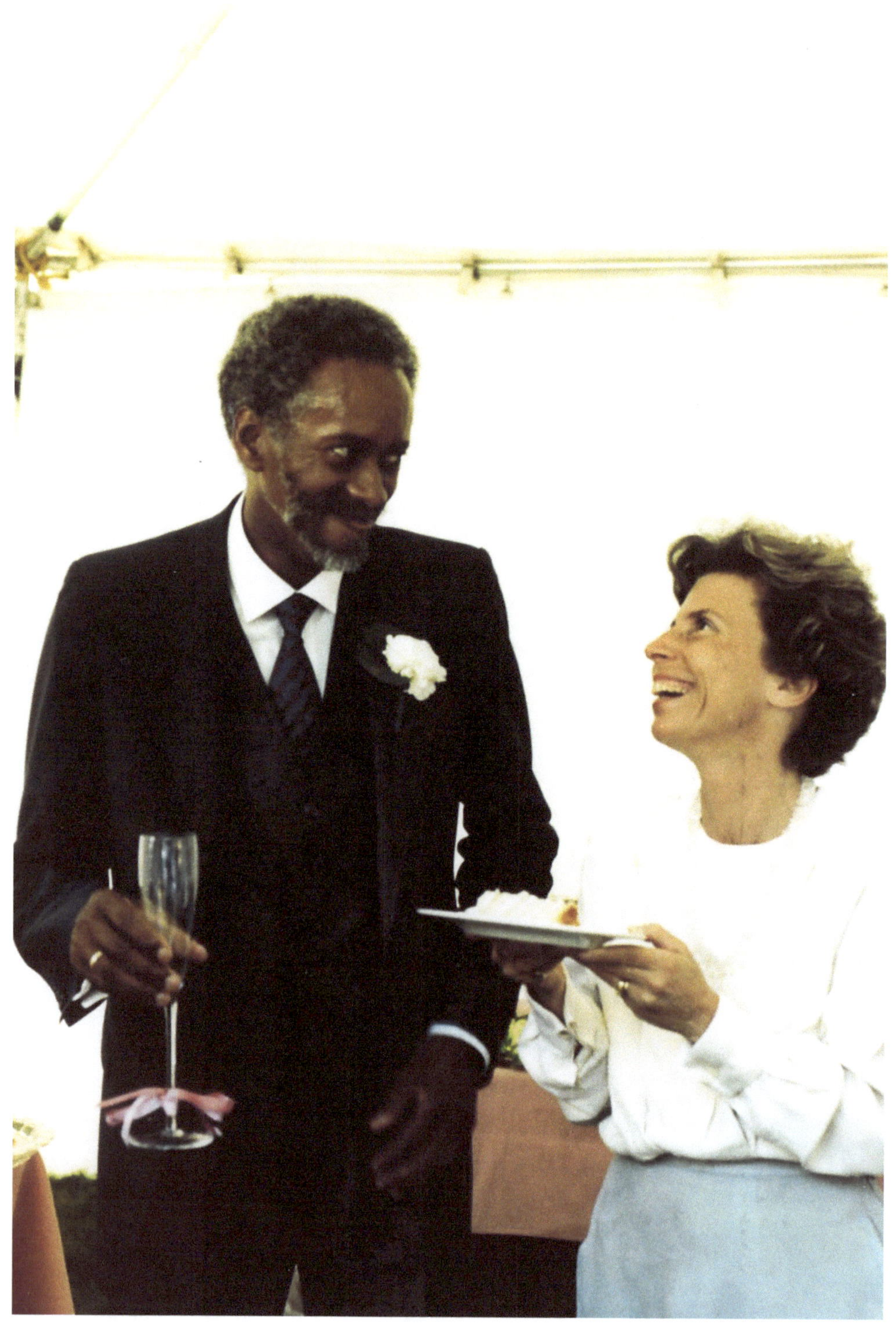

Isabel Taylor offers the wedding cake to Eugene Martin, May 7, 1988

Eugene James Martin (b. Washington, D.C., July 24, 1938 - d. Lafayette, Louisiana, January 1, 2005) was a prolific African American visual artist.

Eugene J. Martin's art is best known for his imaginative, complex mixed media collages on paper, his often gently humorous pencil and pen and ink drawings, and his paintings on paper and canvas that may incorporate whimsical allusions to animal, machine and structural imagery among areas of "pure", constructed, biomorphic, or disciplined lyrical abstraction.

Eugene Martin's works of art can be found in numerous private art collections throughout the world, and are included in the permanent collection of the Ogden Museum of Southern Art, New Orleans; the Alexandria Museum of Art, Louisiana; the Stowitts Museum & Library in Pacific Grove, California; the Munich Museum of Modern Art; the Arthur Schomburg Center for Research in Black Culture, New York; the Mobile Museum of Art, Alabama; the Walter O. Evans Collection of African American Art in Savannah, Georgia, the Paul R. Jones Collection of African American Art at the University of Delaware, the Walter Anderson Museum of Art in Ocean Springs, Mississippi, and the Louisiana State University Museum of Art in the Shaw Center for the Arts in Baton Rouge, Louisiana.

http://www.artnet.com/awc/eugene-j-martin.html

http://www.artstor.org/what-is-artstor/w-html/col-martin.shtml

http://www.youtube.com/nemastoma

www.ingramcontent.com/pod-product-compliance
Lightning Source LLC
LaVergne TN
LVHW070141110826
845147LV00002B/304

* 9 7 8 0 5 7 8 0 2 9 4 0 5 *